T0333547

CHASING FOG

CHASING FOG

FINDING ENCHANTMENT IN A CLOUD

LAURA PASHBY

**SIMON &
SCHUSTER**

London · New York · Sydney · Toronto · New Delhi

First published in Great Britain by Simon & Schuster UK Ltd, 2024

Copyright © Laura Pashby, 2024

1 3 5 7 9 10 8 6 4 2

Simon & Schuster UK Ltd
1st Floor
222 Gray's Inn Road
London WC1X 8HB

Simon & Schuster: Celebrating 100 Years of Publishing in 2024

www.simonandschuster.co.uk
www.simonandschuster.com.au
www.simonandschuster.co.in

Simon & Schuster Australia, Sydney
Simon & Schuster India, New Delhi

A CIP catalogue record for this book
is available from the British Library

Hardback ISBN: 978-1- 3985-2699-0
eBook ISBN: 978-1- 3985-2700-3

Typeset in Bembo by M Rules
Printed and Bound in the UK using 100% Renewable
Electricity at CPI Group (UK) Ltd

MIX
Paper | Supporting
responsible forestry
FSC
www.fsc.org   FSC® C171272

For Dan, Annie, Mum and Dad – who
came with me to find the fog –

and for Seth, Rowan and Eli, always

CONTENTS

. . . and in my fog-self shocked and grey
it startles me to see the sky

ALICE OSWALD (from 'Mist')

Introduction

At first, I didn't find fog – fog found me.

On a gloomy October morning, I drove past a little copse of trees behind a drystone wall at the top of the common. The copse was full of fog: copper bright through the grey, beech leaves shone. I pulled my car into a passing place opposite, hopped out and snapped a photograph on my phone. I'd driven past that copse many times before and never noticed anything but trees. Today, it felt new, strange, compelling.

That Sunday, I took a walk with my husband Dan, our three sons and some friends, clambering up a field and weaving through woods, bound for an Iron Age hill fort from which the countryside opens out all around. A rising fog crept up from the River Severn Valley below, up and over the hill above us, enveloping the woods as we climbed. I lifted my camera from where it hung around my neck and looked through the lens at the fog as it wove through the golden trees. The woods were different: beautiful, but also potent and uncanny. I was sharply aware of the hill fort, invisible in the cloud. Now I could no longer see; its presence (and a sudden vision of the curled figure of a crouched burial found within) loomed over me. All visible traces of the twenty-first century had faded away – the town below in the valley, and even the stile at the end of the path, had disappeared into fog. The landscape became a swirling, changeable space and time felt porous, flowing. My shutter clicked and clicked again, camera binding me tightly to the moment. I was seeing fog as if for the first time – but fog had been there all along.

I spent my early years on the edge of Dartmoor's wilderness, the high, desolate moor a landscape known for its sudden fogs. A ruined castle was my playground, an ice-cold stream my paddling pool. The sun rarely shone on those half-remembered childhood days – skies hung heavy and grey, and my dark hair was always curling, damp with raindrops. My recollections are fractured and imperfect: the rich, earthy scent of the moor, water on my skin, my yellow rain suit, the bite of the wind. Fog was there, too, drifting along the edges.

Now a writer working part-time in a small and lovely bookshop, I once again find myself inhabiting a peculiarly foggy place. I live in a small town tucked under the Cotswold escarpment, alongside the Severn Vale. Some mornings, the fog rises up from the river, moving along the valley and edging up into the streets. On others, it spreads along the escarpment, sinking down the slope and settling among the houses. In the autumn and winter months we can experience several foggy mornings each week. Even on a summer morning, when the sky above me is perfectly clear, if I catch a whisper that fog has risen from the river, I am compelled away from warm sunshine and into damp cloud. To me, fog is an invitation, an enticement, a gift. If I open my window and can no longer see the hill behind my house, I will hurry to the woods with my camera, chasing fog.

Fog is my muse: when I am in it, I see things differently. The known becomes unknown, the familiar unfamiliar. Fog disorientates, blurring the edges of everything – changing landscape, altering colour and softening light. As I walk, I let my camera guide me, looking for shape and silhouette, for secret and story. I see fog as the visual representation of a dream. A foggy morning is rich with mystery and magic, but also with possibility – the everyday feels otherworldly. It is this world transformed that calls to me and I have started to feel that perhaps fog transforms me, too. I share my foggy photographs on Instagram, each one an expression of how I see the world. By typing #chasingfog below each image, I hope to connect with a small but far-flung online community of fog-loving photographers. On a November morning in the densely foggy beech woods, their branches metallic bright, I met an elderly man walking alone through the tree tunnel, staff in hand. He smiled at me, nodded at the camera round my neck, and said, 'It's my favourite time of the year – beautiful, isn't it?' I murmured my agreement and we passed on our ways. In all my foggy walks, I have never seen him since. Inside my phone, other kindred spirits were gathering, leaving comments on my photographs, sharing their own and, on foggy mornings, sending me pictures and messages: 'I woke up to fog and it reminded me of you.' In this small way I felt understood.

Submergence in fog can be an intense experience – it sharpens my senses and I actively engage with all that surrounds me. Stepping into a damp cloud of fog is fresh, cool and enlivening, the closest sensation I have found to the 'zing' that comes from immersing myself in the sea during the coldest months of the year. Fog, like salt water, is completely other – it provides a shock, an escape, a release. My body awakens, and I am outside of myself. I came to love fog because of the way I see, but it also affects the way I feel. Sometimes, unexpectedly, I have found fog in different places – on a Cornish cliff, a Welsh hillside or in a French forest. These encounters fuelled my obsession, birthing within me a wish to trace fog's reaches far and beyond. Fog has many names for its different geographical incarnations, colours and textures: in Wales it is *niwl*; in parts of Scotland, *haar*; on the east side of England, roke. I read these names over and over like an incantation: I gather them as a promise.

Fog is a weather condition that appears without warning and rarely stays for long – I am constantly abandoning plans or taking detours in search of it. Friends will send me fog alerts if they wake before I do to a foggy morning. I have been chasing fog for several years now but my odd pastime has taken on a deeper urgency following the discovery that fog, like so much else, may be under threat from climate change. As a weather condition, fog is disappearing – a 2009 study found that in Europe there had been a 50 per cent drop in 'low-visibility' events (fog, mist and haze) since the 1970s. Around the world, coastal fog is declining, which many scientists believe to be a direct result of climate change. In some areas (such as California) this reduction of fog – with the resultant heat and loss of moisture – could have disastrous consequences for ecology, and for the human population. Fog may be drifting away without us noticing.

INTRODUCTION

If we don't pay attention to fog when it is here, how will we realise if it has gone? Fog is slipping from us, gradually vanishing, and I resolve to chase it, to capture as much of its atmospheric magic as I can. Alone, I cannot protect fog, but I can give it my attention, my devotion. In this book I will seek out fog and tell its stories, setting off on a sensory fog-chasing journey, to the furthest reaches of my foggy imagination. I will travel to a series of contrasting places (from sea to river, mountain to city), each known for a particular type of fog. I'll immerse myself in fog, finding others who love it, and exploring the moods and meanings that we attribute to it: its untold (or lost) stories, its place in folklore, and the way it is visually and descriptively represented in literature and art. This is both a search for the physical experiences of fog and a quest for moments of magic and metamorphosis.

I want to share the wonder and the soothing balm of fog. I'd like to reach out and offer it – a tiny stratus cloud – a chill, fuzzy gift in the palm of my outstretched hand, in the hope that others too will recognise its beauty.

1

WITH VISION OBSCURED – RIVER SEVERN

(Sabrina's veil – inversion fog – sense of sight)

The fog flows up from the valley and slowly, slowly it fills the town. From my little loft-room study window, I watch it edge along the street like a whisper made visible, gently enveloping house after house, until it reaches mine. The huge beech tree in the garden opposite disappears completely, leaving only the echoing calls of its resident jackdaws – ghostly in the viscous air. The world beyond my open window fades to white. I want the fog to drift right in, curl cool tendrils around me and encircle me like smoke. I snatch up my camera, throw my coat over my pyjamas and dash out the door, bound for the woods on the hill. Fog is as transient as it is elusive, and there is no time to waste. On the hill above my house, the foggy woods are hushed and eerie. Puddles on the muddy path catch the dull light. The trees are stark silhouettes; diamond droplets of water glint on their lower branches. I can see only a few feet ahead of me – there is a blanket of silver all around. I smell damp earth and, faintly, the sap of the trees. I'm alone, but the luminous air draws me in. The sound of dripping surrounds me – water droplets fall from the trees with a creeping tinkle. The air is cold and my breath condenses, causing fog clouds of its own. I compose a photograph and the click of my camera shutter echoes.

When air becomes cooled to the temperature at which water vapour condenses into a visible cloud (the 'fog point'), fog forms. It is defined by the *Cambridge Dictionary* as 'a weather condition in which very small drops of water come together to form a thick cloud close to the land or sea'. The irresistible romance of stepping into a cloud at ground level is one of the many reasons why I love fog. Mist, like fog, is a suspension of tiny droplets (at a lower density to fog) and levels of visibility are the only distinction between mist and fog (if there's visibility greater than one thousand metres, it's mist; if visibility is under one thousand metres, it's fog). The terms tend to be used interchangeably – including in this book. But while fog may seem to hang heavy, it is often vital, not static: dipping, waving, seeping, drifting and flowing. Fog is unpredictable – it is not soft and benign like cotton wool. In his 1919 essay 'Das Unheimliche', Freud defined the uncanny as something that is both frightening and yet familiar: the strangeness in the ordinary. This is exactly the effect that fog can have upon a landscape: when it quickly descends, it diso-rientates us, obscuring sight, changing familiar surroundings and making the known world seem odd and unsettling. It was this sensory experience that I felt compelled to explore first: the loss of sight as our vision is diminished by fog's descent; the feeling of a veil being drawn.

A sense of drift and shift is woven into fog's etymology:

appropriately for a word that describes cloudiness and opacity, the origins of fog are not clear. Its widely known meaning is 'a thick mist', but fog also has a more unusual meaning, possibly local to the north of the UK – 'aftermath grass, long or rank grass', or 'moss', which may originate from the Norwegian *fogg* ('long-strawed, weak, scattered grass in a moist meadow'). Fog's origins may stem from another Scandinavian source, such as early Danish *fog* ('snowdrift') or Old Norse *fjuk* ('drifting snow storm'). In Norse mythology, Mist was a Valkyrie, one of a group of maidens who served the god Odin, riding through air and over water to battlefields so as to choose those who will die in battle and those who might live. 'Mist' may have come from the old Norse *mistr*, meaning cloud. In Old English, it was found in the compound words of *misthleoðu* ('misty cliffs') and *wælmist* ('mist of death') – its uncanny nature having ancient roots.

The topography of the area where I live results in more than one variety of fog. On the hilltop above my town, across the undulating fields of the Cotswold escarpment, foggy mornings are common. This is likely to be radiation fog (caused by a mass of unmoving air cooling – and water vapour condensing – as the ground beneath loses (*radiates*) its heat). Fog of this type can linger in high-elevation areas. In the Severn Valley below, inversion fog appears: this occurs in an area of high pressure when air from above sinks down towards the ground, drying out and warming as it falls. The buoyant warm air forms a floating layer over cooler air near the ground surface and fog becomes trapped in the air lower down, as if caught under an invisible dome, like a lid on a jar of cloud. As air in

9

the troposphere (the lowest region of Earth's atmosphere) ordinarily becomes colder with altitude, this represents an *inversion* of expected air temperature patterns. The fog that flows up the valley and into my town has made its way from the river. My fog-chasing journey begins with this fog I know best: the fog that infiltrates my street and life; the fog that first drew me in. I have chased this fog through the woods on the hill, I have chased it along the footpaths, I have chased it through the churchyard, but I have yet to follow it back to its source.

Seen from a peak set atop the woods, beyond the town, the Severn Valley fog that edges up to my window resembles an undulating sea of fluffy clouds. The first time I saw the fog-filled vale from above, it was like stepping into a fairy tale. I stood alone on the edge of the hill at a local viewpoint in front of a crooked wooden gate with a sign reading 'PRIVATE. HANG GLIDING CLUB ONLY.' Beneath me, the land dropped steeply away to flat plains. Roads, fields and villages that usually spread below like a patchwork quilt had disappeared, covered by meringue-pale whirls. The hill opposite floated, marooned in white. In the face of this ethereal sight, I felt exhilarated, but also impossibly small – awed by natural magic. At my feet, spiderwebs sparkled in the dew-sprinkled grass and from the heavens a few sunbeams were beginning to slice through, a reminder that this dreamscape could only ever be temporary. The entire landscape felt new, the ordinary made strange and irresistible. From my briefly omniscient standpoint up on the cliff edge, the fog seemed magnificent, but my perspective would have been utterly different had I been down beside the River Severn, where an obscuring quilt had enveloped the valley.

Wanderer Above the Sea of Fog, an 1818 painting by the German Romantic artist Caspar David Friedrich, depicts a similar scene. In the foreground, a man stands upon a rocky precipice with his back to the viewer. His central position in the painting is the point at which all lines intersect. He wears a frock coat and leans on a walking cane as he looks out across the mystical landscape of a cloaked valley. Other rocky points rise up, islands in a foggy ocean, and at the horizon are the faded outlines of distant peaks on the other side of a canyon. Friedrich's particular way of seeing is inherent in this painting, his use of fog more metaphorical than literal. In the book *Mist and Fog in British and European Painting*, Evan R. Firestone writes that Friedrich leads us 'to the threshold of the unknown'. The artist himself wrote of fog that 'when a landscape is covered in fog, it appears larger, more sublime'. Ideas of sublimity were important to the Romantics, the theory of sublime art having been proposed by Edmund Burke who saw the sublime, the Tate Gallery website tells me, as being 'an artistic effect productive of the strongest emotion the mind is capable of feeling'. Mist and fog – with their unknowability and capacity to terrify and disturb – were considered manifestations of the sublime.

The motif of a figure in the foreground of a painting or photograph viewed from behind is called a *Rückenfigur*. It is a compositional technique that I often adopt when shooting fog – using my tripod and camera remote, I step into the frame and include myself at the front of the landscape, my back to the camera. Yet it was not until encountering Friedrich's painting that I discovered its name. The inclusion of a figure looking out over this landscape gives an indication of the scale of the scene, but it allows the viewer to identify more readily with it too – to make the imaginative leap of stepping into it themselves. We survey the swirling valley along with Friedrich's protagonist but he also obscures our view and we cannot see what his body hides (although it is likely to be fog, obscuring in itself). With his back to us, this figure remains inscrutable. In a 2008 essay, Kathleen Jamie references the trope of the 'lone enraptured male' – a solitary man exploring and finding pleasurable inspiration in wild places. Friedrich's painting could be seen as representative of just this: the figure appears to be male, and seems to be on his own. But we the viewer are behind him, our eyes on his back. So too is the artist, who himself may or may not be alone.

John Berger, in *Ways of Seeing*, emphasises 'the reciprocal nature of vision', the implication being that if the wanderer can see the distant hills, then from the distant hills he too may be seen. We cannot be sure if Friedrich's figure is truly alone and neither can we be certain that he is enraptured. Writing about this painting in his book *The Weather Experiment*, Peter Moore describes the figure as an 'enlightened man' who is 'in control' and not 'dwarfed' by the landscape he surveys. To my eyes, however, he could equally be thrilled and awed by the beauty of nature, intimidated by the scale and wildness of the surroundings in which he stands, or even ambivalent, pausing only for a brief rest. How does he perceive the scene before him? What feelings does it evoke in him? We cannot know, just as we cannot discover what, if anything, exists beneath the painting's sea of fog.

Back down in the Severn Valley (hidden as I stood on the peak), fog is experienced not from a safely contemplative distance but with immediate intensity – it is visceral and all-encompassing. Here, fog can fall quickly and unexpectedly, blocking out the sun and drastically reducing visibility. Roads become treacherous, but so too does the river. On 25 October 1960 – an autumn day that had begun with a sunlit morning – a heavy fog fell suddenly across the wide River Severn. It was the end of the day and the estuary was busy with vessels on the evening tide bound for the docks at Sharpness. One of these was a tanker barge called the *Wyesdale H*. Chris Witts, a sixteen-year-old working as deckhand on this barge, later wrote that the unexpected fog was so thick 'it was impossible to see the bow from inside the wheelhouse'. The crew's vision became quickly obscured; all recognisable landmarks disappeared, and if the Severn navigational lights were lit, they could not be seen. The deckhand was sent to the bow to listen for the Sharpness foghorn, in order that the skipper could orientate accordingly. The fog was so dense that the other vessels on the Severn had become invisible to them until almost within touching distance. The *Wyesdale H* briefly passed close to its twin, the *Wastdale H*, a barge carrying a cargo of petroleum spirit. The deckhands of the twin barges spoke briefly to one another as they emerged and then vanished back into the fog.

Also in the fog listening for the Sharpness foghorn was the *Arkendale H*, a tanker barge carrying fuel oil. Like the other barges, it was owned by John Harker Ltd (each named after a Yorkshire dale followed by the same identifying suffix). By the time the mast lights of the *Wastdale H* and the *Arkendale H* appeared out of the gloom, the two barges were so close that it was already too late for their respective skippers to steer them apart, despite best efforts. Collision. Locked together, the heavy barges were taken by the tide as the current pulled them up the river towards the Severn & Wye Railway Bridge, striking the bridge sideways on. The bridge partially collapsed directly onto the barges, which, due to their cargoes, burst into flames, as did the surface of the river. Visible from the shore as a red glow, the resulting fire was so intense that the sky was lit through the fog. Five men lost their lives that day, in what would become known as the Severn Railway Bridge Disaster.

A newspaper report from the *Bristol Evening World,* published the following day, relates the events of 'a night of horror in nil-visibility fog'. George Thompson, skipper of the *Arkendale H,* recalled 'the roar, the blinding flash and searing heat' as the barge 'erupted into flame on the fog-shrouded river'. A few days after the accident, on Sunday 30 October, small charges were detonated in the sinking vessels to prevent them from drifting any further. The railway bridge, never repaired, was dismantled in the late 1960s, but the river keeps its secrets – traces of the bridge piers are visible at low tide, and so too are the wrecks of the *Arkendale H* and the *Wastdale H,* lying side by side, forever locked together in the Severn mud.

It is oddly resonant that the clearest view of these wrecks can be seen from Purton Hulks – a ships' graveyard. Here, along the bank of the Severn – where the river runs parallel with, and close to, the Gloucester and Sharpness Canal – eighty-six ships of varying size and age (barges, schooners, trows and docklighters) have been 'hulked'. These vessels were not accidentally wrecked, but deliberately beached: released at high tide so as to be carried up the riverbank, after which holes were made in their hulls so that they filled – first with water, and then silt – thus strengthening the bank and protecting the canal from the encroaching, erosive power of the Severn. This unusual tidal erosion barrier was initiated in 1909 by the canal company following a collapse in the riverbank, and the final boat was added in 1965, just a few years after the Severn Bridge Disaster.

On the day I go to look for the wrecks, where the canal path forks off towards the ships' graveyard, I notice a pink wave of rosebay willowherb, also known as fireweed. The tide in the Severn is almost completely out, and a goods train whistles as it thunders past along the other side of the river. A sign reading 'Final Resting Place' lists the names of the purposefully hulked boats. Everlasting sweet peas bloom up through the long grass, and spiky flowers of Clematis vitalba (commonly known as Old man's beard) intertwine with brambles. The Purton Hulks come into view – massive concrete barges emerging out of the bank, half sunk into the mud and covered with swishing grasses. Along the riverbank, numerous carcasses of wooden boats sink, rotting, into the earth, rusted metal ribs piercing through the grass. I've been here many times over the years – my children have run along these paths, exclaiming over each newly discovered boat and listening for the trains. I remember, as a child myself, visiting the site of a different ribbed boat carcass – the Anglo-Saxon ship burial at Sutton Hoo. What might an archaeologist, several hundred years into the future, make of these boat sacrifices? What would they see at Purton Hulks? The last remaining signs of some ritualistic boat cult, perhaps. Without the explanatory sign, these deliberately sunk hulks would not appear so different to the accidental fog-sunk wrecks of the two barges in the centre of the river, all their stories gradually being subsumed.

I'm alone today, and it feels unearthly, the Severn's history visible on the surface. Along its edges, the mud is dotted with the tiny footprints of gulls. Looking out to the centre of the river, I can clearly see the wrecked barges, jagged and rusted, rising from the sandbank. From this angle, only the *Wastdale H* is fully visible, but I've seen drone footage that shows the two barges lying close together, touching in the mud. A plaque has been erected to commemorate the fiftieth anniversary of the disaster. It is dedicated 'to the memory of the five crew who were lost, the three survivors, and the many gallant rescuers who together played a part in the tragic events of that fateful fogbound night'. Mounted onto an original bridge stone, the plaque is illustrated with pictures of the intact bridge, and the barges, seaworthy as they were before the fog fell that night. This peaceful place must have been truly horrifying on that fateful day in 1960 – the fog, the fire, the explosion, the sirens and the screams.

As I walk back through the hulks, the tide is coming in fast – I watch it rising quickly up the sides of the wrecked *Wastdale H* and *Arkendale H*. Soon they will be swallowed again by the Severn, as they are every day, the surface of the water closing smoothly over them. The breeze blows and the fireweed flickers. A couple of summers ago I spent a day travelling this stretch of canal parallel to the river on my parents' narrowboat. Bound for Sharpness, at the end of our trip we passed languidly between two tall stone towers – the remains of the swing-bridge that would have carried the trains from the Severn Railway Bridge over the canal. My dad told us then the story of the disaster, and pointed out where the Severn Railway Bridge would have traversed the wide expanse of river to our starboard side. It was a slow day on the canal, the sun glistered the surface of the water and a swan paddled silently past. All was calm, with only the sound of crickets. But even on a sparkling day of clear visibility, beside the Severn the possibility of fog is never far away. As on the day of the disaster, weather here can change in a matter of hours. Today, it's possible to see for miles, across the river and beyond, and yet in no time at all this landscape could disappear – familiar landmarks and navigational markers there, but suddenly invisible.

There is a more mythical explanation for the dreamlike Severn fog – folklore tells that it originates from the Celtic river goddess Hafren, also known as Habren and renamed by the Romans as Sabrina. In his *History of the Kings of Britain* (c.1136), Geoffrey of Monmouth told Hafren's story: her father, King Locrinus, concealed his daughter and her mother (his mistress Estrildis, a 'striking beauty') away from his wife Gwendolen in an underground cave. It was Gwendolen's father Corineus who had forced Locrinus to keep his promise to marry his daughter (despite his professed love for Estrildis), and when Corineus died, Locrinus left Gwendolen and made Estrildis his queen. Gwendolen – furious – raised a Cornish army, killing Locrinus in battle and seizing the throne. Hafren and her mother were thrown into the river and drowned by vengeful Gwendolen, who ordered that the waters should take the girl's name – in Welsh, Afon Hafren; in English, River Severn. In some subsequent versions of the story, young

Sabrina, spiralling down to the depths, was caught and kissed by the river spirits, making her a goddess. Local legend tells that since Sabrina's drowning, the changing river has reflected her capricious moods.

John Milton was intrigued by this figure, weaving her into his masque Comus. In his retelling, when the 'gentle nymph' Sabrina is cast into the water, the spirits of the river reach up to her, draw her to them and revive her – a 'quick immortal change', making her goddess of the river:

> The water-nymphs, that in the bottom played,
> Held up their pearled wrists, and took her in

Milton's Sabrina is gentle, with powers to undo the spiteful magic of 'clasping charm' and 'numbing spell'. She is sympathetic to the plight of women: 'swift/ to aid a virgin, such as was herself'. In years past, young girls are said to have left offerings to Sabrina beside the river, in hope of her aid. Milton's goddess extends her blessing across and beyond the river valley, venturing forth as daylight fades and she 'visits the herds along the twilight meadows'. Those hazy hours of dawn and dusk are when she makes her presence known. In one folkloric retelling of Sabrina's story, she 'is most strongly felt on those misty mornings' – in the dawn mist, her spirit temporarily leaves the river, returning only 'when her veil of mist is lifted by the sun.' On those mornings when the fog moves up the valley, the spirit of the river goddess is abroad.

The River Severn is the documented location of an even more unusual and mystical weather condition than Sabrina's billowing fog – a fogbow, which is a meteorological phenomenon formed in a similar way to a rainbow: appearing when sunlight encounters fine water droplets contained in fog, mist or cloud (which have a considerably smaller diameter than raindrops). The droplets diffract the light, broadening its reflected beam, meaning that a fogbow is usually white in appearance. In 1798, another of the Romantic painters, Joseph Mallord William Turner, portrayed one of these white rainbows arcing over a Cumberland landscape, reflected in Buttermere Lake below. In his painting, *Buttermere Lake, with Part of Cromackwater, Cumberland, a Shower*, the awe-inspiring power of nature evokes the sublime. In January 2022, a photographer taking pictures of a house on the Portishead coastline noticed a fogbow arching across the blue sky, over the spindly tower of Black Nore Lighthouse. Dashing to the beach with camera in hand, he captured a beautiful image of this rare occurrence, which 'appeared to start in the River Severn and stretched all the way across to Portishead'. Caught on camera, rather than canvas, the fogbow is nevertheless stunning; its diffuse and ghostly arc, rising up from the River Severn, may have been Sabrina's most magical gift yet.

The philosopher Walter Benjamin suggested that if our eyes rest on a natural object (such as a mountain or a tree) at a distance, we see it, we interact with it and we are exposed to what he called its 'aura'. I recognise this sensation. When I stood above the undulating sea of fog, my sense of the power and unpredictability of the natural world was palpable – fog's unsettling visual and emotional influence could certainly be described as its 'aura'. I can only imagine that, seen in person, a fogbow would leave a lasting impression – this unusual meteorological event an experience that would transcend the purely visual. To witness one would seem, I think, like a blessing. Benjamin also considered a work of art to have an aura (the manifestation of its uniqueness). He saw auras as being 'withered' by reproduction, meaning that the image of *Wanderer Above the Sea of Fog* I see in the pages of a book is not the true painting, and that a photograph of a fogbow, while stunning, cannot convey the full visual power and tangibility of its original aura. In apparent agreement with Benjamin, John Berger wrote that in an original painting the paint becomes imbued with 'stillness and silence', which closes the 'distance in time between the painting of the picture and one's own act of looking at it'. Standing in the Hamburg art museum looking at Friedrich's original painting may therefore be the only way to experience its aura, just as being physically present in the foggy landscape, or glimpsing the fogbow with our own eyes, may be the only way to truly experience the aura of the fog.

Whenever I take my camera out on a foggy morning, what I seek to capture is the way that fog feels: the mood, the story, the physical and also the emotional landscape. If fog's aura is impossible to replicate, I hope to evoke its emotional resonance. Berger wrote that 'the photographer's way of seeing is reflected in his choice of subject', and in the same way that Friedrich's way of seeing is reflected in his painting, every picture that I take of the fog says something about who I am – embodying not only what I see, but also the particular way in which I see it. My pictures encompass my response to the fog, which, like this mercurial weather condition, shifts according to mood. The goddess Sabrina's moods, if reflected by the river and the fog, must be similarly changeable. I recognise that my interest in chasing and photographing something that has the power to obscure me may also somehow reveal me. Yet fog's tendency to block our vision also means that every image of fog, made with camera or with paintbrush, will conceal as much as it reveals – there is always something unseen, hidden behind.

In summer, fog is infrequent, the lanes around the Severn River Valley lined with hogweed and meadowsweet, flourishing in areas where the water levels rise and fall. The cloying scent of the flowers drifts in through my open car window; a sign reads 'Shepperdine and the river', and I take the turn. I have come in search of the Shepperdine Lighthouse and the keeper of the lights. Percy Palmer was the last full-time lightkeeper of the Severn's twenty-one navigational lights, 'which cast their warning beams on the estuary from the Lower Stone Beacon to Berkeley Pill'. This stretch of river is one of the most hazardous waterways in the British Isles, with its fast-descending fogs and the second-highest tidal range in the world. In the days before automation, when Percy took the job, the keeper of the lights had to keep the Severn lights burning using paraffin and bottled gas.

The road ends abruptly and, as I pull over, I see nothing but sky ahead of me. A slope leads up towards the river, at the top of which two cyclists have alighted from their bikes and stand, taking in the view. They survey the same expansive vista that I took in from high on the peak, but on the day I stood above like the Wanderer, this spot down beside the water would have been submerged by fog. Today the Severn levee is clear, grasses along the river swishing like a quiet etymological echo – a reminder of the alternative meaning of 'fog'. In the distance, I see the two Severn bridges, cars moving slowly across like beetles. The surface of the river is muddy brown and uneven. Clouds are low, grey and slightly frothed, but there's not a hint of fog – visibility is almost perfect. I'm looking upstream in the direction of where the two barges crashed in 1960, and though I can't see that far, in a waft of breeze from downstream I faintly smell the sea.

The Severn is a wide river, almost a mile across here. If fog dropped I would be able to see almost nothing, certainly not across to the opposite bank, where today the fields are lit up by the sun. Skylarks are calling and there's nobody here but me. A little Meadow Brown butterfly rises up from the grass and flies off in the direction of where I think the lighthouse must be . . . and another, and then another. I follow, passing through a gate and continuing along the thistle-lined path at the top of the levee. I can hear crickets among the purple flowers and, as I grow closer, the mechanism on the lighthouse spinning. Even in the daylight this lamp is lit and glowing, ready for darkness or descending gloom.

This modern light mast is not a romantic sight – a squat red and yellow box rests on a short tower with a metal platform above it. An instrument spins on the top, and facing the river is an electric light. Behind it, some distance from the water, is a metal pole topped with a second light. This Range Rear mast replaced the elegant metal 1906 lighthouse tower in 2010, but the original lighthouse keeper's cottage remains – a pretty white building with arched windows, set back from the river. This is the White House, tied cottage of the Severn

Light Keepers, where Percy Palmer and his wife Olive lived as Percy kept the lights.

In the local community, Percy was said to be legendary for his fearlessness. His duties involved manoeuvring lighting oil drums, climbing perilous ladders on pylon towers, and skilfully bringing his rowing boat alongside lighted buoys in the estuary, tasks he performed in all weathers – including, of course, fog. A true man of the river, who kept the lights for sixty-five years, a clipping from an unnamed newspaper shared by the local museum quotes Percy as saying he was 'pickled in the Severn': his memories went back to the days of trows carrying corn and coal, and to barges '"linked like strings of sausages" moving slowly behind towing tugs.'

Once, a 3,000-ton cargo ship fell victim to the fog's swift descent over the Severn, becoming disorientated in the sudden gloom. Despite the low visibility, which would have hidden the navigational lights, this ship escaped the tragic fate of the *Arkendale H* and *Wastdale H* thanks to Percy, who stood on the riverbank and shouted instructions through a megaphone to the pilot and skipper, allowing them to beach safely on a sandbank, to be floated off on the next flood tide. Thanks to his courage and his detailed knowledge of the river, the keeper of the lights was himself a beacon, guiding the ship to safety.

Today, gulls are tiptoeing across the sandbanks. The tide is on its way out, more and more shoreline mud becoming visible. Further along the river is a stretch of rock where my children and I often go in search of crinoid fossils, looking closely along the murky tideline for tiny prehistoric stars that we pull out of the dirt and gently clean to a shine.

It was my friend Rich Edwards, an artist local to the Severn who captures its fog in his paintings, who first told me about the keeper of the lights. He suggested that I visit the Saxon church of St Arilda's in the village of Oldbury-on-Severn, where Percy is buried. Leaving the levee behind me, I pass the Anchor Inn and a community shop and I buy three bunches of purple sweet peas from an honesty-box stall for a pound each. St Arilda's is built from warm reddish stone and sits on a small hill, surrounded by its graveyard and overlooking the River Severn in the valley below. As I shimmy through a kissing gate into the churchyard, I see Oldbury Power Station in the distance, a sailing club, the patchwork of fields beside the river and the Severn bridges, closer now.

I'm following the instructions of Meg, from the local history society, to try to find Percy's grave. I walk up and down the rows of gravestones, the church above me and the Severn below, the wind in the grass and the trees, looking for his headstone. The grass is long around the edges, dotted with thistles, convolvulus, buttercups, clover and vetch. Meadow Brown butterflies are here too, flitting among the flowers. I try counting the grave rows, but my calculations aren't quite right. I count again, scrutinising grave after grave, and just as I begin to think that perhaps I'm not going to find it after all, here it is:

IN MEMORY OF OLIVE MARY LOUISE PALMER
DIED 15TH NOV. 1974
AGED 74 YEARS.
LOVINGLY REMEMBERED
BY HER HUSBAND PERCY

AND OF
PERCY GEORGE PALMER
HER DEARLY BELOVED HUSBAND
DIED 15TH FEB. 1992
AGED 90 YEARS.
KEEPER OF THE SEVERN LIGHTS FOR 65 YEARS.
NOW RESTING IN THE ETERNAL LIGHT.

At the top of the gravestone is a carving of a lighthouse. Not the metal tower that stood next to the White House, but the traditional tall coastal building. The headstone is covered in lichen, but you can see the lighthouse quite clearly, embossed into the stone. Beams of light are etched, and at the bottom of the lighthouse are steps carved in rock, leading up to the stone door. I want to reach out and touch it, but I stop myself. The lichen is mottled black and white, with a smattering of glowing yellow. There is a flowerpot in front of the grave containing nothing but dead grass. I wish that I had thought to bring something with me to place here, and then I remember the flowers I bought from the stall, and I return to the car to collect a bunch of purple sweet peas to leave with the keeper of the lights and Olive, his wife.

From where they rest you can see the river, almost as far down as the White House and the lighthouse beside it. I think about Olive Palmer and I try to imagine how it would have felt watching her husband – who picked her posies of wild orchids – go out into the storm-tossed river with its fierce tides, time and time again, creating a safe path down the river that would be otherwise unseen, and risking his life to light the lights. Olive's perception of Severn fog would presumably have been very different to my own. For her, the swift descent of fog, destroying visibility across the river, must have represented close and present danger. In the newspaper cutting about Percy, it explained that he was a keen fisherman, catching flatfish, whiting, shad and soles 'bigger than the Shepperdine Sunday collection plate'. 'My wife and I,' he is quoted as saying, 'aimed to have fish every day for tea.' When the fog came down, and Percy set out to light the lights, did Olive wait and watch for him on the riverbank, did she join him in the boat or was she cooking a fish supper for his return?

Leaving Olive and Percy's grave behind, I walk up the steps into the top of churchyard where the oldest graves sit, close to the church walls. Above the door is a statue of St Arilda. She, like Sabrina, was a virgin and is said to have been martyred – murdered – by a man named Municus when she refused to 'lie with him' nearby. Inside the church it's musty and silent – there's no one here but me, and the sunbeams through the glass recall to me Philip Larkin's high windows with their ability to comprehend the sun. One of these windows is a stained-glass representation of St Arilda who floats, weightless in the coloured air, while behind her spreads the landscape – a vista of the Severn framed not by a camera's viewfinder or an artist's canvas, but by the church window. Looking inwards I see, on the church's stone floor, her image dissipated into jewel-bright pockets of liquid light. If the murdered Sabrina became mist, the murdered Arilda became light – both now seen, and yet unseen. But a change of state is no consolation for a life cut brutally short. I buy a couple of postcards, close the heavy door behind me and step back out into the wind. Over the fields beside the river, I spot a buzzard. Wings barely moving, it circles, floating in the air currents. I watch it rise, spiralling higher and higher as it drifts along the field.

On summer evenings, this churchyard is ashine with glow-worms, and it seems fitting that the keeper of the lights should have his final resting place in a churchyard lit by their luminescence. The name is a misnomer – they aren't actually worms but beetles, and it's the wingless females that glow, to attract flying males for mating. In July, St Arilda's Church turns off its floodlights to preserve the darkness and help the glow-worms find each other. I return to the churchyard at dusk one day as the sun sets over the river valley and Sabrina's twilight meadows are a swirl of lilac and gold. The tide is in, the sky deep blue fading to black, a rough-hewn cross is silhouetted against the sunset, and there's a waxing gibbous moon. The only sound is a flag flapping loudly on top of the church. Standing in a churchyard waiting for dark to fall feels strange and counterintuitive. I look around me, hoping to see the pinprick shine of a glow-worm's light. A couple of times I think I glimpse one, but it's just the last of the sun illuminating a blade of grass. I have seen glow-worms in the late dusk before, in Normandy lanes on family holidays, and am hopeful that I will see them this evening. I've read that the best time to spot them is between ten o'clock and midnight, but by half past ten night has almost fallen and I'm not brave enough to stay on this lonely hill until it's pitch black. As I leave the churchyard, I see the shadow of a black cat padding silently through the gravestones.

September comes, and the fog suddenly returns, as my artist friend had told me it would. Opening my kitchen door one morning to feed the chickens – the touch of holiday sun lingering on my skin – I look up in the direction of the hill, but see only a mass of pale cloud. Without pausing even to boil the kettle for tea, I set off along the valley to the levee. Where the cyclists stood on my last visit is now just a blankness of sky, an absence of colour. Clematis vitalba climbs the wall beside the ramp, fronds in between flower and fluff. Alongside the path, a bank laden with plump blackberries, and two hawthorn bushes hang heavy with red. The damp air is deliciously cool on my face after weeks of dry summer heat. Stepping out onto the flatness of the levee, I see the river enfolded with soft fog – Sabrina's veil has fallen and I can barely make out the far bank. The sky is heavy and uniformly grey, dropping down to the Severn, where the tide is out. In the distance someone stands beside the water – a tiny silhouette. I wonder if this enigmatic figure could be a fellow fog lover, but – like the Wanderer – they are inscrutable.

A flock of gulls curls up from the river, where a navigational buoy is just visible through the gloom. Narrowing my eyes to focus, I catch a glimpse of two flickering lights in the direction of the opposite bank. Downstream towards St Arilda's, the Severn bridges are almost invisible and the power station is a blurred silhouette. I turn to look upstream towards Sharpness (and the site of the accident) but can see no defining features, only a sweep of river that merges at the horizon into sky. In front of Percy's cottage, the Range Rear light is lit, its solid glow facing out towards the foggy river. Wood pigeons coo, mud crackles, I hear gulls in the middle of the sandbank. Perhaps my eyes are adjusting, or maybe the fog is gradually fading, but an outline of the opposite bank is emerging in hazy layers, like a distant mirage. My gaze is drawn back to the yellow square of the lighthouse, constant and comforting in the glowering morning. Pulling my cardigan around me, I turn and head for home. The figure on the sandbank remains, facing down the river to the sea – alone again in the fog.

2

MY FOG-SELF – DARTMOOR

(pixie-led – hill fog – sense of self)

The moor calls to me.

I spent my early childhood in a town called Okehampton, at the north-west tip of Dartmoor National Park, a place where grey stone echoes grey sky, and the air is almost always damp – at least in my memories. Our house was a converted barn at the edge of town, on the road to the castle (the supposedly haunted ruins of a medieval motte and bailey, surrounded by woods), which sits above the River Okement on Dartmoor's margins. I was a child of moor, mist and wind. I splashed in icy streams, hid in hollow trees, and ran across blustery hillsides. I existed for much of that time inside a cloud of drizzle – perpetually in the weatherspace between rain and fog. The moor's wildness sings to me, fluttering at the edges of my consciousness, and as the years pass, I have felt the increasingly acute pull of its raw beauty. It occurs to me that my strange urge to chase fog – my desire to immerse myself in damp and grey – may originate from Dartmoor's siren song.

One day, in a charity shop near my Gloucestershire

home, rifling absent-mindedly through a box of maps, I discover, tucked at the back, an old Ordnance Survey map of Okehampton and North Dartmoor. It's an unexpectedly serendipitous find – Dartmoor is over a hundred miles away, and the rest of the box's contents are walking guides to my local area. I buy the map and spread it across my desk, looking for familiarity, studying the contour lines, trying to match map to memory. Place names tug at my mind. With my finger, I trace the boundary of the Dartmoor National Park, a line that snakes directly between my childhood home and the castle on the side of the moor – an invisible division between everyday and wild. I search for rooms to rent on Dartmoor and find one in a remote cottage belonging to a woman named Storm. The moor's call becomes impossible to ignore and I click 'book', deciding to take an autumn trip. Dartmoor is known for its sudden fog, which – according to folklore – can be summoned by the local pixies. I will travel to Dartmoor to look for this fog, but I also know that I will somehow be looking for myself.

We have been experiencing the warmest October on record and where I live fog has become unexpectedly elusive. There have been fewer foggy days than ever, and not just in my experience – the community of fog photographers I have found on Instagram are also bemoaning its absence. In anticipation of my fog-chasing trip, I've discovered a Dartmoor webcam, not far from where I will be staying. It shows me the view at co-ordinates 50.57°N, 3.94°W facing North, 369 metres above sea level – a place called Powdermills, near Princetown. The camera is trained on a field edged by a wire fence, with a wooden gate and a stile. At the end of the field – in the middle of the picture – is a windblown tree. Its lower branches have been stripped bare of leaves, presumably by the sheep that now graze on the other side of the fence, straying out towards the moor beyond, alongside an occasional Dartmoor pony – those distinctive, hardy creatures that roam, semi-feral, across the moor. The changing positions of the animals are the only discernible movement shown by the webcam, but when it rains, fat droplets appear on the camera lens. In the right of the picture, a ruined stone building can be seen, and further into the distance is a clump of trees, some rocks, and the high and distant moor. Whenever I sit down at my desk, I click on the webcam, the slowly changing landscape oddly soothing from the relative warmth of my study. I have never been to this particular spot on Dartmoor, but there is nevertheless something familiar about the colour of the stone, the texture of the sky and the twist of the tree. Each morning, before I begin to write, I check the webcam. Each day, I am waiting for fog.

Dartmoor fog finally falls on a Wednesday in late October. I click on the webcam, expecting the usual view of fields with distant moor behind, but the landscape has been subsumed by fog. The tree in the foreground is visible, its leaves a mixture of green and bronze, but behind it, all is blurred. There are the fading silhouettes of three more trees along the hedge, and beyond them nothing but a bank of fog. The moor has completely gone and the camera lens is rain-splattered, with not a sheep or pony in sight. Even from the other side of a screen many miles away, this fog feels disorientating, and I shiver. Against all reason I find myself zooming in to the image, as if I might catch a glimpse of a Dartmoor pixie in the mist, but the snippets that shine in the grass are just blown leaves. I wonder – ridiculously – whether I could make it down the motorway, across the moor to this remote, unknown foggy field and return in time to pick up my smallest son from school, but common sense prevails. I study the weather forecast but can see no mention of fog for this place. Perhaps pixies really have conjured it. As I continue to check the webcam image over the course of the day, the fog thickens until even the trees in the background disappear from view. They do not reappear before nightfall, when the screen fades to black.

November comes and I set off for Storm's place. As I drive over the first curving stone bridge and cross the peaty River Dart, I let out an involuntary whoop of excitement. This place is a part of me – I took my first steps on ground not far away. In autumn, Dartmoor's colours are warm and inviting – the last of the yellow oak leaves cling to the trees and the hills are dappled with swathes of bracken in tones of rust. I drive along narrow lanes, past freely roaming ponies and sheep contained by a network of drystone walls. Among coconut-scented gorse bushes and scattered rocks, a lichen-dusted Methodist chapel teeters on the edge of the hillside. The road climbs on, up and up, to the top of the windswept tor, where a lone tree stands gnarled and tiny. Sun and dark clouds dance endlessly together across the sky, flashing patches of light onto the moor valley below. I find Storm's stone cottage down a rocky track, on the valleyside above the river – I am staying in the annex. Outside my window sheep stroll past, and the Dart rushes on through day and night. There has been a storm – the river is high, flushed with rain and the internet is down. I have no phone reception and I am alone in this unfamiliar, isolated room on the top of the moor, but Dartmoor's wilderness feels like home to me.

I have arranged to meet my best friend Annie for a swim at Foggintor Quarry, a disused granite quarry that has carved a hollow gash into the outcrop that was once Foggin Tor. I am hoping, of course, that this place will live up to its name and offer up fog, but although I am an experienced winter swimmer, I am nervous about swimming in such an isolated spot in November. We walk together along an old tramway that leads to the quarry, initially built to allow granite to be taken to Plymouth in horse-drawn trucks, and then later used to carry steam engines and coaches to nearby Princetown. The landscape here tells of its industrial heritage: along the path we find flat stones with the clear indentations of rails. This quarry was in operation for over a hundred years, supplying granite for London landmarks including Nelson's Column, as well as for Dartmoor Prison, just a few miles away. Families once lived here and I can make out the site of the old Foggintor School down by the road, now a lonely walled car park called Four Winds. We pass a slumbering spoil heap of discarded stone and the jagged ruins of cottages, hollow windows like empty eyes framing trees and hills beyond. The entrance to the quarry would be easy to miss – a path to our left vanishes into a narrow gap between two rock faces. We clamber across and stop, stunned; an expanse of water sparkles below us, surrounded by sheer, steep cliffs. There are little islands, covered with tufty reeds, and below the surface of the water, large lumps of stone are clearly visible. Hard granite, the core feature of this unique landscape – a composite of feldspar, mica and quartz.

I strip down to my swimming costume and pull on neoprene boots. Wind ripples across the surface of the water as I make my way gingerly in. It feels temperate for November, and once I am over the stones I strike out and swim towards the granite cliff. This is a secret, special place, like nowhere I have swum before. Back when it was a working quarry, quarrymen and their families would swim here, and later – half a century ago – there were repeated rumours of mysterious figures glimpsed in the quarry at night. Dubbed 'the shadow men' by locals, they must have been a truly unsettling sight, rising from the murky dark. It later transpired that these were soldiers on secret practice missions (a large swathe of Dartmoor is a Ministry of Defence training area). Shades of the many past swimmers seem to drift by me, flitting across the surface of the water. Today, in autumn sunshine, the pool is empty and calm. The rock face glistens, ferns grow from the cracks, and rivulets of water run down its patterned surface, dripping like the sound of impending rain. It towers above me as I float on my back, looking up at lowering clouds that almost touch the clifftop. I will them to drop and cascade down, submerging me in a waterfall of moorland mist. Closing my eyes, I concentrate on the sensation of water holding me up. I can hear wind, and echoing calls of crows. The sun touches my face and I think of how submergence in fog would feel different to submergence in water. Unlike the clarity of this water (its depths fully visible), fog is obfuscating. Although it is, of course, just water in another form. The deep, cold quarry pool is sharply anchoring. I feel held and present – contained by the place and tied to the moment. I am floating free, in the midst of the moor, far away from the places I usually have to go; far away from the person I usually have to be.

As I swim, flashes of sunshine come and go, clouds rolling in and away again, the weather changing moment to moment. Clambering out, I spot a scattering of white quartz shards along the path. Pulling my towel around me, I gather a few, pushing them down into the pocket of my bag. Sitting on a rock with a flask of coffee, granite rough on the backs of my legs, I pick up a piece of reed from the water's edge and absent-mindedly split it with my fingernail, opening it out to reveal the foam within. The gesture is unexpectedly familiar and a childhood memory prickles at the back of my mind, sharp like the tip of the reed against my skin. Aware that we must keep moving and stay warm, we pack up our things and walk to the far side of the quarry, where the stepping stones of the path have been covered by water. My foot slips and wets my boot to the ankle, cold soaking through my wool socks. Clouds darken, and a rainbow arcs briefly across the sky. It's a gift, but also a warning – seconds later rain comes, fast and heavy. We clamber hurriedly up, over granite boulders and along a sandy sheep path that winds up the hillside. By the time we reach the tramway again, the rain here has stopped, but the far hills are misty strata where it falls beyond. Puffball mushrooms grow alongside the old rails and Annie points out a kestrel hovering steady above the path. Its wingspan is no-ticeably smaller than that of the familiar pair of buzzards that live on the hill behind my house. We stop to watch as it waits effortlessly in the air above a tangle of gorse. When it finally swoops, in a series of rushing drops, it flies to the bottom of a drystone wall and grasps its prey, carrying it up and away, riding thermals into the distance.

On Dartmoor, a search for fog is inevitably also a search for pixies. Local folklore tells of travellers on the moor being caught in a sudden, inexplicable, disorientating fog conjured by pixies – small, fae sprites who make their home on the moor. The pixies weave a mischievous misty spell, and to be caught in this fog is known as being 'pixie-led'. They were not the only supernatural creatures on Dartmoor who could conjure fog to disorientate travellers: a cave below Vixen Tor was once believed to have been home to a gaunt and towering witch called Vixiana, who would summon a thick fog, luring travellers off the path in order to perish in a bog. But while some suggest that the pixies too were attempting to lure unsuspecting folk into one of the moor's dank bogs – where hummocks wave with fluffy white 'pixie-grass' (Eriophorum or Cotton-grass) – William Crossing (a prolific chronicler of Dartmoor, who died in 1928) countered: 'May it not be that [travellers] are merely being drawn away from ground regarded by the pixies as theirs?'

Perhaps the pixies and the witch used the unearthly Dartmoor fog as a magical way of protecting themselves and their spaces – a warning to stay away and avoid parts of the moor far from current human habitation. In the confusing event of being pixie-led, suggested solutions included: emptying your pockets out, turning your coat inside out, and, if you can find one, drinking from a fairy spring – all of which are said to break the pixies' spell. Although Ruth E. St

Leger-Gordon wrote in *The Witchcraft and Folklore of Dartmoor* that 'the true Dartmoor pixie has long since vanished into the mists and mires where he properly belongs', being pixie-led is not necessarily a thing of the past. Speaking on the *Countryfile* podcast in November 2021, author and Dartmoor dweller Tom Cox described his experience of being caught in the fog: 'It happened to me, I got pixie-led.' Despite his familiarity with the route, and having since re-examined the map, he said, 'Dartmoor spun me round and I still can't make head nor tail of that.'

Annie, herself a Devon dweller, tells me that the best place she knows to look for pixies is Wistman's Wood. This rain-soaked ancient oak wood is one of Britain's last remaining temperate rainforests. Its name may derive from the Devon dialect word 'wisht' (meaning uncanny or 'pixie-haunted') and it was believed to be a haunt of the Wisht Hounds – a pack of demonic black dogs that roamed the moor accompanied by a Wild Huntsman (said to be Old Crockern, ancient spirit of Dartmoor, or even the Devil himself). After warming up from our Foggintor swim with lunch by the fire in a small hotel, the two of us walk the track to the wood, along the Dart River Valley, through bracken and rugged moorland. Track turns to boggy path – almost a stream – and we tiptoe from stone to stone. Wistman's Wood is visible from far away – holding tight to the side of the valley, a dense cluster of trees, leaves ready to drop. I later read in *The Lost Rainforests of Britain* that evidence suggests in the past Dartmoor was blanketed by 'extensive temperate rainforest', but today only a few tiny pockets of knotted, mossy oaks remain. We pass rocky outcrops which, when I look at the map afterwards, I see are the remains of hut circles. I am reminded of what Robert Macfarlane terms the 'tingle of connection, of walking as seance'.

'I almost feel we might meet someone medieval passing through the trees,' Annie tells me, and I sense it too. Time is different here – raw and ragged, the path tearing into the landscape, allowing the light of the past to slip through.

Along the hillside above Wistman's Wood lies an ancient way, known as the Path of the Dead, or the Lych Way. In medieval times, it was expected that burials should take place in the parish churchyard of the deceased, and nowhere else. In the local Parish of Lydford – at that time the largest in England – there was a collection of isolated homesteads known as the Ancient Tenements, which lay in the valleys of Dartmoor, around a dozen miles away from their parish church. When a resident of these tenements died, their shrouded corpse had to be carried by cart across the moor – a long trudge across rough ground, in often inclement weather – for burial in the distant Lydford churchyard. Douglas St Leger-Gordon imagined that 'when the death-white mist crept down from the heights and wrapped the cold wide Moor in its spell of unreality and stillness, all the phantoms of Wistman's Wood must have mingled with the procession'. Even in fading golden sunshine I feel a shiver at the thought of a lonely, weather-beaten funerary procession passing just above where we stand. To make such a long and mournful journey through the chill Dartmoor fog must have been fatiguing and quite possibly terrifying.

Wistman's Wood is a tranquil place on a windy hillside, a timeless forest. The gnarled, stunted oak trees are wrapped with green, their boughs plaited together in an ancient embrace. Feathery ferns and candyfloss clouds of lichen hang from their branches. There are over one hundred species of lichen in Wistman's Wood – including incredibly rare Horsehair lichen – and these epiphytes (plants that grow on other plants) offer a clear sign that this is no ordinary wood: it is rare and precious temperate rainforest. On the woodland floor we see jumbled large, flat, white-speckled rocks and mossy boulders, the damp-loving, spongy moss recalling fog's possible botanical etymology. A huge stone forms a ledge with an open cavern beneath it – a place for pixies to gather, or perhaps druids. Wistman's is a wildwood, a sacred grove that according to folklore was once frequented by druids – some suggest its name connotes 'wise man'. We stand on the edge of the wood, looking deep into its green shade – it's too fragile now for us to explore far between the trees, as Annie did in childhood.

I hear the lowing of cows in the field that borders the wood, the cawing of crows and the brisk splash of the ever-running Dart at the bottom of the valley. I reach out to touch a brittle oak leaf. The air smells of moss, cow dung and the freshness of rain. Low now, the sun flickers behind the trees, and then, across the sky floats the clatter of distant gunfire. The sound recalls us to the heightened awareness that we cultivate when out on the moor – our quiet respect for this landscape and our endless monitoring of shifting weather and light. This bewildering, isolated place is different to the familiar woods and fields where I walk at home, not least because its inconstant weather can be unpredictable and dangerous. Rain or fog could suddenly fall, and we are mindful of the approaching dark. At once I feel ever so slightly afraid, and we hurry back along the side of the valley. The orange sun sinks down below a drystone wall, and a final volley of gunshots echoes as we emerge with relief by the road.

Just as the Severn Valley fog can be observed from St Arilda's, St Michael de Rupe is a vantage point from which fog can be seen moving across Dartmoor. A small medieval church that sits on the top of Brent Tor, it perches above the earthwork remains of an Iron Age enclosure, at the west-ernmost edge of the moor. This is a forlorn, windswept spot to have built a church. Legend tells it came about because a wealthy merchant once found himself caught in a dreadful storm at sea. He prayed to his patron saint, St Michael, for deliverance and vowed that if he was spared, he would build a church on the first and highest point of land that he saw and dedicate it to the saint. At once, the storm winds dropped and the ship was saved. The merchant was as good as his word – and while it seems unlikely that Brent Tor could have been the first point of land visible to him from the coast, it has been suggested that it can indeed be seen from Plymouth Sound, and that the lower-lying lands may have been hidden by fog, causing the tor to rise up into his vision like an island.

Some versions of the story say that it was the Devil himself roaming the moor who created the storm. Enraged by his failure to sink the ship, when he saw what the merchant was creating, he seized the man's building materials, throwing them down at the base of the tor. Day after day the merchant would carry his materials back up the tor, and night after night the Devil would scatter them – until one night he arrived to find St Michael himself atop the hill in the blackness. The saint flung a granite boulder at the Devil, who, turning to escape, was hit on his heel. The merchant was left to finish his church in peace.

The next day, in search of a foggy view, I follow a path that snakes up the hill, through the bracken to the dark-grey stone church. A flight of shallow steps leads to a gate that clicks behind me. A couple of trees cling to the hillside, their branches heavy with hanging clumps of the lichen I saw in Wistman's Wood. A pale nest of it blows across the path and I pick it up to study it. The interwoven threads remind me of hair or seaweed – soft and tangled. It is gentle green, like a calm ocean on an overcast day. (Later, when I look it up, I find that it's of the Usnea genus, sometimes called beard lichen.) I push the weighty church door and it creaks open slowly. Inside is dark and silent, but outside the wind batters the walls. A stained-glass representation of St Michael fills the window above the altar – beyond him, the moor. Bell-ringing ropes hang unmoving, and a sign says: 'Other men laboured and ye have entered into their labours.'

Even without the Devil's involvement, the building of this isolated church would have been quite an undertaking. The wind blusters and wails through the keyhole as I pull my coat tighter and step back out into it. Gravestones balance on the edge of the churchyard, crustose lichen forming whirling cloud-patterns on their surface. Cloud hangs heavy over the farmland, and on the distant moor beyond, the tops of the tors are lost in white – submerged, I presume, in fog. From here you could stay and watch fog sweep over Dartmoor – bouncing from tor to tor, enveloping hill after hill, and then flowing away again. I make my way back down the steps, my eye on those cloud-topped tors.

When does cloud become fog? When does murk become mist? I had thought that chasing fog would give me a clearer understanding of what it is, and where to find it, but as I search, distinctions are becoming blurred. The way to the prison is where I find my first Dartmoor fog – or perhaps fog leads me to the prison. As I climb a steep road on top of the moor, cloud drops further and further until it's touching the ground and drifting across the landscape, and then it is not a cloud any more – this is fog. I pull my car into an empty lay-by to take a photograph. My camera snaps, the fog drifts on, and there – towering out of the greyness – suddenly rises the foreboding, hulking height of 200-year-old Dartmoor Prison, seemingly the foggiest place on Dartmoor. The prison's high granite walls glow with lit windows: long rows of small bright squares, outside which the fog swirls. It's an ominous, Dickensian sight, although the well-known novel that mentions an escaped convict from 'Princetown Prison' is Arthur Conan Doyle's *The Hound of the Baskervilles*, which is believed to have been partially written in the old Duchy Hotel nearby. I have packed a copy in my bag to read on this trip, but in the lonely lay-by the thought makes me shiver. For one moment, I am fully enveloped in fog – but it's gone in an instant, floating on past the prison, then fading away.

Poet Alice Oswald, who lives in a village beside the Dart (her 2002 poetry collection named after the same river), wrote a poem called 'Mist' in which she describes her 'fog-self' – the person that she becomes during a foggy interlude – a self drawn into, and entranced by, the fog. She is astonished, first by the mist as it falls and then afterwards by the reappearance of sky. Yet there's an implication too that fog becomes a part of her, perhaps even beyond this time of enveloping: her 'soul gets caught in it'. When I first read the phrase 'fog-self', it rang in my mind with bright clarity. I too have a fog-self, I realised. The person I become when surrounded by fog is a nebulous, hazy, free and drifting version of myself. I can't be sure whether I am my fog-self only in the fog, whether she is a permanent facet of me, or whether she – like fog itself – is always a little beyond my grasp. I am not myself in the fog but seduced and remade by it. Could I – as the last twist of drifting fog catches me up and releases me again – be permeable to fog? On a cold foggy morning, when I breathe out in clouds, I see my breath mingle and become mist. At the same time, as fog's dampness wrinkles my skin and soaks into my hair (making it curl tightly), I intuit that a little of it is now within me. My body contains water and some of that water was once fog – I have inhaled fog, absorbed it, become in part fog. The fog by the prison fades and I continue on my fog-chasing journey, but now I understand that I am searching also for myself – it is my fog-self that I'm seeking.

In *The Hound of the Baskervilles* (which I read that night in one sitting, curled under a quilt in the lonely cottage, surrounded by inky moor), Dr Watson arrives on Dartmoor in autumn. He senses in the countryside 'a tinge of melancholy', and is told that a convict has escaped from nearby Princetown – which, as I turn the pages, is just a few miles away. He describes the moor's 'vastness' and its 'grim charm', noting the prevalent evidence of prehistoric habitation and suggesting that this can cause you to feel pulled into the past, to 'leave your own age behind you'. In many ways, Dartmoor is unchanged since 1901, when Arthur Conan Doyle visited Princetown and wrote his famous book. It remains a vast place, where the dead have left echoes, and legends prevail. It seems likely that the 'enormous coal-black hound' at the centre of Conan Doyle's novel could have been inspired by tales of the Whist Hounds. Also central to the novel is the Dartmoor fog, which is so vividly realised that it is at once both a place and a character. The novel's denouement occurs at night by Grimpen Mire (a swampy bog, perhaps based on the Bronze Age settlement of Grimspound, combined with Fox Tor Mire), over which there hangs a 'dense, white fog':

> The moon shone on it, and it looked like a great shimmering icefield, with the heads of the distant tors as rocks borne upon its surface.

This wall of fog appears to have its own agency: Sherlock Holmes describes it as 'the one thing upon earth which could have disarranged my plans'. He and Dr Watson watch helplessly as a sea of fog draws closer, threatening to completely overwhelm their vision as it drifts, curls and eventually – menacingly – crawls: '... the fog-wreaths came crawling round both corners of the house and rolled slowly into one dense bank ...'

In the end, the fog aids, not hinders Sherlock Holmes – it proves to be the undoing of the spectral hound's murderous master, who becomes lost to the mire in Dartmoor's foggy dark, while Holmes and Watson remain in the 'white wool'-wrapped house until morning. The moon-shimmered fog proved ungovernable, and even the sharpest of minds was forced to wait until it finally lifted for a search to begin, so that the story could draw to a close.

In the morning, the first thing I hear is the bubbling Dart. It's flowing too fast for me to safely swim, but I walk down to dunk myself in one of its pools. I hang my clothes on an oak, clover leaves clustered around the base of its trunk, and lower myself into the water. Splashing cold wakes me. Afterwards, sipping hot coffee, I spread out my Dartmoor map and pore over it. Scattered with hut circles, tumuli and stone circles, this is a landscape where the people of the past feel close and present, as if it might be possible to hear their voices just out of sight, over the next hill. At its centre, the map shows mostly contour lines, streams and tors – on paper, the middle of the moor appears desolate, but I know it to be full of life and raw beauty. I touch a familiar moorside village with my finger – Belstone. Closing my eyes, I am five years old again, running along the edge of the moor. Fog calls me to Belstone because on the village website I found a photograph from 2018 of a rare fog-based phenomenon called a Brocken Spectre, seen and recorded by a Belstone resident. The image shows a cloudy, mist-covered moor. In its centre is the towering shadow of a giant, crowned by a rainbow aura – a Brocken Spectre. This unusual visual occurrence appears only when conditions are exactly right. If a walker stands on a hill or mountain peak partially enveloped by fog, with the sun behind them, their magnified shadow can become cast in mid-air onto the cloud, creating a huge, shifting shadow-self with a rainbow crown called a glory (the sunlight interacting with the water droplets). A Brocken Spectre is both self and other, a dark shade with an angelic halo. It's an unreal apparition – a visual manifestation of the interplay between self and fog – the ultimate, multi-faceted fog-self. I do not expect to see my own spectre here (although I dream of it), but I am nevertheless pulled to this place.

As I walk into Belstone – a pretty village that opens out onto the moor, overshadowed by a tall tor – the familiarity of its elegant houses drags my heart up to my throat, and layers of memory peel suddenly away. As a young child, I played here for a few summers with a green-eyed boy. Our parents were friends – as we chased, they laughed and chatted, watching our games from The Tors pub, the tables of which spill out onto a green that leads straight to the moor, spreading down into the valley where a stream runs through. Looking back at those days fogged by the passage of time, I recall sensations: toes chilled by peat-brown water, wind tangling my hair, the sound of my father's laugh, chinking pint glasses, racing clouds. It was an untamed place, different to the park in town, and we children also felt untamed – delightedly lawless and free. Now, on this day in autumn as I stand at the edge of the village, there are sheep dotted on the distant hillside, the sky is ever moving and leaves flutter across the grass at my feet. A flock of birds rises up from the moor. This is a place on the cusp of the wild – land of bracken and bone.

Twenty years before I played here as a child, the poet Sylvia Plath took riding lessons on a horse called Ariel at a riding school nearby. Plath lived for a little over a year in North

Tawton, a village on the edge of Dartmoor next to Bow, the village where I lived as a baby. She died on my birthday, and although it was years before I was born, the happenstance of date and place has long plucked at my thoughts. Ariel was both the name of her horse and the title poem of her poetry collection, a poem written on her thirtieth birthday, just months before her death. While living in North Tawton, Plath also wrote the first drafts of another poem about horse-riding on Dartmoor, a poem she eventually called 'Sheep in Fog'. Set on the December moor, with its speaker riding a rust-coloured horse, this poem has a mood so sombre that Plath's biographer Heather Clark writes: 'seldom has the existential threat of depression been so memorably aestheticised'. As Clark notes, the fog in this poem causes the hills to disappear, creating a disorientating landscape. It is an unsettling portrayal of Dartmoor's fog, heavy with hopelessness. I find it disquieting to think that Sylvia Plath may have ridden some of the paths I now walk, and fog offers a point of connection. When I am in fog, I feel out of time – if fog fell on this corner of the moor, it wouldn't be hard to imagine the dolorous clopping of the hooves of a rust-coloured horse.

I am wearing a wool coat, itself the colour of rust. I catch a glimpse of my reflection in a house window and see that my hair is curled more tightly than ever – full of the damp Devon air and yesterday's fog. The wind blows fiercely as I make my way to the top of the village, through the gate onto the moor in search of the Nine Maidens – a Bronze Age stone circle. It is located off the path and I struggle to find it, but when I eventually stumble across the stones, I am awed. Windswept and remote, this circle of stones stands strong atop the moor. Although there are more than nine in the circle, folklore tells that the stones were once nine maidens who ill-advisedly danced on the Sabbath, and so were turned to stone and condemned to dance every noon for eternity.

As I stand among them it's just past noon, but although the wind is fierce, the stones are unmoving. I walk slowly around the circle, startled by a perception of its deep meaning and inherent power. Passing through this circle is the St Michael's ley line, one of the 'fairy chains' of interconnected sightlines first described by Alfred Watkins in *The Old Straight Track*, a book that begins by reflecting on how we can feel ourselves strongly drawn to the long-ago dead, who 'felt no strangeness in sun and wind and rain' and – I would add – fog.

On my way back to the village, I unwittingly stray – there are many narrow paths, the ground is boggy, and for a while I lose sight of the stone wall that I had been carefully keeping on my left. Even in daylight, without a murmur of fog, it is bewildering. An old gorse bush creaks loudly in the wind and, for a few moments, panic rises. As I find my feet back on the path, I notice a lone figure on the moor walking parallel to me, and although he is doubtless just a rambler, I am unsettled and hurry back to the village before our ways cross. I leave my muddy boots at the door of The Tors, and step into the warm, chatter-filled bar to eat a bowl of parsnip soup in my wool socks. The draught cider in this pub of my childhood memories is called Devon Mist.

In many ways, the moor remains unknown – exposed and expansive, its core far from roads or current human habitation.

Aside from walkers, locals (and in certain areas, the military) few people step into this space, and the ways to traverse it can be hard to follow. Fog too is an unknown – so when fog falls on the moor, a collision of mysteries creates an utterly unknowable space. Perhaps inevitably, it's at Foggintor that I experience the full whiteout of Dartmoor fog, stopping there on my way back from Belstone. Once again, I walk the tramway to the quarry, but this time I can see just a couple of metres in front of me – beyond my next steps is nothing but featureless white. Beside the path, sheep shine in the fog like little lights. I pass the puffball mushrooms that I noticed previously and they shine too. Fog drifts across the path, wind whistles past my ears and the air smells clean as it whips my face. I'm completely alone – I can't see my car; I can't even see the road anymore. It's just whiteness, the moor, me and the sheep. I am reminded, as I always am when I see sheep in the fog, of the Plath poem – her sheep are implied, never explicitly described beyond their mention in the title, and yet the poem is infused with their pale glow. I read of an old belief held by Dartmoor farmers that a kind of changeling sheep could sometimes appear among a herd. Not easily distinguished from the other sheep, except to the knowing eye, an 'elemental or malignant spirit' was believed to have assumed the form of the animal. Although the sheep here are benign, almost comforting, there is something in their unexpected brightness that suggests the spirit world.

I am grateful for the tramway to follow – a waymarked path through the gloom. I take one step at a time along its stones, knowing that without it I would be utterly lost. I now regret the words I said in jest as I walked here in the sunshine – jokingly goading the pixies, asking them to bring me fog. Fog has fallen, I can see nothing, and pixies no longer seem cute imaginary creatures. They imply power – something primal that belongs to the spirit of the moor. As I step through the gap in the rock that leads to the quarry, the fog clears for a moment, and I am struck once again by the quicksilver unpredictability of the weather here on Dartmoor – it is one thing to set off in fog and find yourself in clarity, but would be quite another to set off in clarity and suddenly find yourself in fog. The wind whips in across the side of the quarry, leaving rough waves on the water surface. Below my feet, the peaty ground is speckled with white quartz. It would be a different experience to swim here today – at the far end of the quarry, swirls of cloud drift in; a sweep of fog is moving past the top of the walls and filling the space, making the air thick and uncertain. Fog is coming in, and Foggintor Quarry is living up to its name. High atop the hill above the quarry, a white Dartmoor pony is grazing. It stands, silhouetted against the sky like a figure from a fairy story, unearthly in the falling fog.

When fog obscures our vision, white is the colour that can be seen most clearly. In the past, across Dartmoor's bogs, fragments of china clay were set down to mark ways of safe passage in the dusk. Those broken pieces, luminescent in the twilight, recall the shards of quartz that I collected beside the quarry, cool splinters that when I return home I pile on the bookshelf beside my bed. From dark granite comes gleaming quartz. On my last night in the cottage, at the top of the hill in the blackness, a full November moon is hanging over the horizon, silvery and soft. I think of Plath's moon above the yew tree, seen from her window that overlooked a churchyard not far away. The moor is lit by moonlight, and lit by white things that show the way – white ponies, white sheep, white clay, white quartz. Perhaps the white things that shine in the fog can lead me not just to the path, but to myself. Often my fog-self too shines – when I go to shoot self-portraits in the fog, myself the *Rückenfigur*, I wear a white dress. It allows me to be seen more clearly in photographs, but also to weave myself into the moment, to drift as the fog drifts, to glimmer in the gloom.

Now, on the moor in my rust-coloured coat, I have a sense of where I came from – of who I once was; of deep memory. Wildness hums in my blood and essence of fog floats through my body. I see beauty in bleakness and this has taught me to push on even when I am afraid, to embrace coldness, to not fear emptiness. I believe that here – a land untamed and free – I am home. This landscape knows more of me than I ever knew of myself; has always known things that I am only now beginning to discover. I am vulnerable here – nothing on the moor is within my control – but there's a thrill to this, to my acceptance of it. The person I believed myself to be is not as real as the person I know I am in this place. I don't understand this in my head but I recognise it in my bones. On the moor, I know myself most fully, and here in the fog, my fog-self is closer to my true self than anything I have yet experienced. There is a strange clarity that comes from embracing the unknown, and I recognise now that this too is what I have been looking for – I chase fog, but the unknown is also what I seek.

*

A week after my Dartmoor trip and the Foggintor swim, I arrive at my regular weekend swimming spot to find that the quarry there has filled with mist – a witch's steaming cauldron – the air above bubbling, the deep water below endless and black. Climbing down the steps, I lower myself into both water and mist. The far end of the quarry has disappeared, only the arms of distant swimmers can be seen, rising and falling in endless elegant arcs. Mist spirals up from the water like plumes of smoke. I stretch out my arm towards it, but each time it vanishes before I can touch it. The sun turns ripples gold, and the surface of the water glitters – a sequinned dress beneath a misty cloak. I am enveloped by it, and yet it is always just beyond my grasp. My fog-self delights in this elemental immersion of cloud above, water below. It feels thrillingly primal to dive into a wild unknown. I stay, floating, until the absence of feeling in my limbs tugs at my thoughts, reminding me that the moment of ease when I start to melt, lulled by the water's numbing embrace, is past the time to pull myself back to shore. Slowly, I climb the steps, skin tingling, shaking drops from my shoulders and fingertips. I have returned to land and to life, but my fog-self is still out there. She floats in the quarry, she drifts across the moor, she hides behind the trees in the wood on the hill. She is a mist-wraith, a thing of breath and cloud – forever waiting for me.

3

Lost in the Fog – Meirionnydd, Wales

(niwl – mountain fog – sense of direction)

We take the mountain road to Aberystwyth, winding through the rain. After a week of fierce winter storms, the River Wye is in flood – flowing down the hillside ahead of us, a whirling cascade. Below in the valley it has burst its banks, washing across fields. For miles we've been following a rainbow, a full arc spanning the damp green countryside. Now, we seem to drive right under it – one end of the arc falling into trees on the hillside, the other dipping down into the torrent. The rainbow's colours appear to swell and brighten as we pass beneath, but once the road climbs up into the mountains it fades and disappears.

When I asked my husband, Dan, to join me for a few days weather-watching in Wales, my intention had been to chase fog atop the mountain Cadair Idris, but we now find ourselves at the quicksilver heart of a storm's aftermath – in the midst of a changing weatherscape. These unpredictable storms are unsettling – looking for meaning in weather, as I now do, I interpret their heightened intensity as a frightening indication of our changing climate. Eventually, the sun finds its way out of the clouds, its touch most welcome. We snake up through the Cambrian mountains, following the road as it clings to peaks and sweeps through valleys.

This mountain range was once rich in gold – as well as silver and lead – mined as far back as Roman times. Now, the derelict mines of the Cambrian Mountains orefield have been colonised by plants, including mosses, lichens and rare ferns such as forked spleenfort and moonwort (named for its half-moon-shaped leaves and once believed to be a magical plant with healing and alchemical properties). We pass close to a disused mine, and I find myself twisting the gold band on my fourth finger – my Yorkshire granny's wedding ring, bought by my grandad from a jeweller friend for their wartime wedding. Granny always told me it was 'Welsh gold, like the Queen's', but the story of its true provenance is now irretrievably lost to the past. With my focus on the sense of direction, it is stories of the lost that I am here for, and our first destination is the National Library of Wales, in search of a mythical king, foggy mountain rescues and spirits of the mist.

The library – 'home to the story of Wales' – is an imposing stone building that stands on top of a hill overlooking Cardigan Bay. We are welcomed in out of the squally wind and I am sent up two flights of stairs to the reading room – a hushed space with vaulted ceilings, cathedral windows and teardrop chandeliers. Around the edges of the room are floors of alcoves with oak bookshelves, but in the centre, above rows of desks, emptiness stretches up and up to the ceiling's full height. I love libraries – the quiet, the musty scent of books, the palpable presence of captured knowledge – and this is one of the most magnificent I have visited. This library – repository of secrets and stories – is somewhere I hope to find what was lost. A stack of reservations waits for me at the central desk and a librarian shows me to a small computer room, where I can view the archive footage I have requested. In this book-lined space all is serene, but out beyond the tall windows crashes the wind-stirred sea.

It was a book that led me here, one that takes its name – *The Grey King* – from the Brenin Llwyd, a folkloric figure known also as the Monarch of the Mists. *The Grey King* is the fourth book of Susan Cooper's fantasy novels, *The Dark is Rising* sequence – books that I began as a child and then found myself strongly drawn to when I read them to my eldest son. *The Grey King* is set in what Cooper described as: 'a piece of mid-Wales, around Cadair Idris, on the southern edge of Snowdonia' (now Eryri), adding that 'part of me is always there'. The author's grandmother was born nearby in Aberdyfi (where her parents also lived for many years) and although she settled in the USA decades ago, Susan Cooper clearly feels a strong connection to this part of Wales. She writes that her books are 'full of the history and geography of the British Isles, their time and place, their people and weather and skies and spells'. Cooper's deep sense of landscape – and deft exploration of time, magic and myth – is what gives her novels enduring power, and this particular book has tugged at my mind for years now, twisting its way into my imagination. Weather, skies and spells are exactly what I hope to find.

In *The Grey King*, Cooper describes Cadair Idris as being

the dominion of the Brenin Llwyd, a dark and malicious king of the mist – his breath a cold grey fog of tattered cloud, hiding the mountaintop from view. Although Cooper tends towards a creative interpretation of the mythic elements within *The Dark is Rising* sequence, in this book she makes a distinction between fiction and folklore on the first page – following notes about geography, she writes: 'the Brenin Llwyd I did not invent', a nod to the book's folkloric roots and, to me, an invitation. I feel compelled to visit this mountain, in search of its fog-weaving king.

The Brenin Llwyd, wrote Marie Trevelyan in her 1909 study of Welsh folklore, sat 'among the mountains robed in grey clouds and woe to anybody who was caught in his clutches!' People, especially children, who strayed too high onto the slopes risked being snatched away by this terrifying individual, who approached the unwary in stealthy silence. The Brenin Llwyd was not confined solely to Cadair Idris – stories about him were told across the mountainous districts – and he was a figure that inspired fear and awe. He appeared 'on the hill sides, just where the clouds appear to touch them', but this king didn't merely seek the clouds – the Brenin Llwyd was thought to be able to control them, having the power to 'direct the mist's journey through the air'.

Also associated with the Brenin Llwyd are the Cŵn Annwfn: spectral hounds of Annwfn (the Welsh Otherworld). Not unlike Dartmoor's Wisht Hounds, these beasts are part of the Wild Hunt – a recurring folkloric motif that takes many localised forms, the Berkshire version of which (led by an antlered horseman called Herne the Hunter) appears in Cooper's *The Dark is Rising*. The Cŵn Annwfn too are led by a shadowy magical huntsman – known as Gwyn ap Nudd. He was considered to be a king of Annwfn, and of the Tylwyth Teg (the Welsh 'fair folk'). Like the Brenin Llwyd, this king was prone to snatch unsuspecting mortals, leading his Wild Hunt in pursuit of human souls: to hear the baying of the Cŵn Annwfn was believed to be an omen of death. Gwyn ap Nudd was favoured by the Brenin Llwyd, welcomed into his 'court of mists', and the Brenin Llwyd was said to have joined him in a hunt with the hounds of the Cŵn Annwfn on the slopes of Cadair Idris. It has been suggested that the Brenin Llwyd and Gwyn ap Nudd could in fact have been equivalent characters – two facets of the same cruel folkloric king.

My own first sight of the mountain comes in grainy black and white. In the side room of the library, I watch clips of silent film footage – 'the old county of Meirionnydd'. The film is fast, and there are crackles on the screen that look like dust, or perhaps they are the flash of raindrops. In the foreground, a drystone wall, a gnarled blossom tree in full bloom and, towering in the background, Cadair Idris. The tree shudders and blossom drifts in the wind, but the mountain's presence is solid and unchanging – Cadair Idris exists not only in the past or present moment, but also in deep time. Some of the rocks that make up this mountain were created when lava erupted on the sea-bed millions of years ago; others were formed by the slow build-up of sediments – strata of rock containing layers of time. The film flickers and skips, the camera pulls back, and the full height of the mountain becomes visible, its greyscale summit wreathed by drifting cloud – the breath of the Brenin Llwyd? When I see Cadair Idris in reality the next day, I will discover that the colours of the mountain are rich and its surface is textured, layered with rock, bracken and winter-bleached tufty grass. As we set off to climb it, we will round a corner to see it rise up ahead of us, slopes mottled in shades of green, russet and deep, faded purple – angled with trees and sprinkled with sheep. At the very top of Cadair Idris (I will note with equal parts trepidation and excitement), fog floats.

Seen from below, fog on the mountaintop is a romantic sight, but I know that it can reconfigure the landscape – dulling the light, obscuring the path, and making it unexpectedly difficult to maintain a clear sense of direction. Cadair Idris is a place where people do get lost in the fog. Before our trip, I study reports of rescues on this mountain. I read of walkers who reached the summit but found that fog fell and they were unable to locate the correct path down; of others who became stranded halfway up in deteriorating weather and poor visibility, and of those who were found and rescued, shivering and disorientated. Here, the lost are rescued by the Aberdyfi Search and Rescue Team, trained volunteers who provide a year-round search and rescue service, night or day. Occasionally the Coastguard helicopter is brought in to transport the injured, but should they be too high in Cadair's cloud, even the helicopter cannot reach the summit and the rescue team must bring the casualty part-way down the mountain to be airlifted.

In the library I watch footage from a 2004 BBC documentary about mountain rescues on Cadair Idris. On screen, at the foot of the foggy mountain, the team prepare to take part in a helicopter rescue training drill. They are wriggling into waterproof trousers and high-visibility jackets emblazoned with 'search and rescue', checking off a list before piling into the helicopter that will take them further up the mountain. 'A mountain highlights extremes: if the weather's beautiful, there's no better place to be – if the weather's bad, there's no worse place to be,' the mountain rescue team leader says to camera. 'If somebody's lost on Cadair, where do you start? It's a big area. It becomes a little like a detective game, really.' Searchers in waterproofs fan out, walking away into the fog, gradually fading from view.

The art of finding those lost in the fog requires skills in navigation and mountaineering, knowledge and experience of the mountain terrain, a dose of common sense, and perhaps an occasional sprinkling of intuition. It also calls for teamwork and trust: the most experienced rescue team members have known each other (and the mountain) for decades. To find your way on any mountain – particularly in fog – you will need more than just a sense of direction and a good map (although both are essential). In *A Field Guide to Getting Lost*, Rebecca Solnit describes the necessity of paying attention to 'the language of the earth'. She suggests that those who do get lost when out walking may have exhibited a lack of attentiveness to 'the thousand things that make the wild a text that can be read by the literate'. Her language of landscape requires walkers to closely observe their route and landmarks, looking forwards as well as back. Noting the location of running water and the position of the sun is important, as is remaining attuned to the weather's shifting mood. But as someone who actively seeks it, I know that fog is extremely hard to predict – difficult to find, yes, but also difficult to avoid.

'Weather can change quickly and unexpectedly in the mountains, so be prepared to turn back if conditions are against you,' the Search and Rescue team advise in a local information leaflet. Recognising the moment in which it has become prudent to turn around and retreat off the mountain is crucial, particularly in the event of fog, and yet this is also the point at which it becomes evident that the once-trodden path looks different on the way back down. Nan Shepherd wrote in *The Living Mountain* that not getting lost on a mountain in the mist is 'a matter of the mind' – lost being a state that can be avoided by those who carry a map and compass, and who remain calm and clear-thinking, even as the world turns to white.

It is January, a challenging time of year to climb a mountain, and we have been poring over the forecast for days. The morning after our visit to the library, we wake in a cheerful red converted railway guard's van on a hillside in Meirionnydd. Rain bounces loudly off the corrugated roof but I open the window to the morning air. A marcescent leaf twists on the beech tree outside, and I note wet beard lichen on its branches – the air here has the pristine clarity of altitude, scented with petrichor, woodsmoke and coffee. Beyond the carriage is a field with two goats who nibble grass by the fence and strip a low-hanging tree of its bark; below them a farmhouse and then nothing but trees. Looking out over the valley below, I observe snatches of drifting low cloud – little puffs of fog. I curl up under the duvet again, to re-read *The Grey King* for a few minutes, while Dan walks down the hill to fill a basket with more logs for the stove. Smoke from the chimney spirals up and is lost to the wind.

Today, we plan to walk up on Cadair Idris and I am bubbling with nerves – my research into mountain rescues has ensured that we are prepared, but I am also now deeply aware of the unpredictability of January weather and our relative lack of hillwalking experience. As we wait for the morning rain showers to pass over, we set off into nearby Machynlleth for supplies. Dan goes to buy food, and I duck into a bookshop. 'I'm sure I've spoken to you before,' the lady behind the counter says warmly as I buy a couple of cards. 'I recognise you, you're very familiar.' I tell her it's my first visit here and she replies, 'You must have a doppelganger.' I don't know whether to be unsettled or charmed at the uncanny thought that I might have a double somewhere in this unfamiliar town – perhaps my fog-self is more corporeal than I imagined.

Mountains are not comfortable terrain for me. I am confident in woods and fields, on hills and even the moor, but a mountainous landscape inhabits a different scale to the ones that I know. I feel both intimidated and exhilarated by the day ahead. Place names hold stories too, and Cadair Idris is a mountain with a formidable name: its meaning is 'Idris's Chair', and legend tells that Idris was a giant – one so huge he used this mountain as a chair on which to sit and oversee his kingdom. Formed by glacial erosion, Cadair Idris has a distinctive shape – a scooped, bowl-like formation known as a cwm (or corrie), with steep, curved cliffs rising above a deep lake in the valley bottom – the outline of the cliffs resembling an immense rocky throne. Idris's legend may refer to a medieval king of Meirionnydd known as Idris Gawr (Idris the Giant), who was thought to have spent time atop this mountain, possibly studying the stars.

It is said that if you sleep overnight on the slopes of Cadair Idris, in the morning you will either wake as a poet, you will never wake again, or – in the bleakness of the lonely night – you will have become mad. On this mountain it seems there is more than one way to become lost; in the fog you may lose your way, but brave a night under the stars, and you risk losing your mind. I attended a talk by mythologist and storyteller Dr Martin Shaw, who then alluded to the fact that as a young man he slept for four nights without food on a hillside near a Welsh mountain. In a more recent interview, he named that mountain as Cadair Idris. For him, something fundamental happened there. 'I entered the mystic,' he has said of that time. Now he mesmerises audiences with his words – a true poet in the bardic tradition – but concealed within (and transmitted through) the stories he tells is the depth of his life-changing epiphany on Cadair Idris.

We are cautious and it is not until patches of clear sky start to appear that we make our own way to the mountain. The steep Minffordd Path will take us to our destination – we are walking to Llyn Cau (the deep lake at the base of the cwm), in which I am hoping to take a brief dip if conditions hold. This glacial lake is like a hidden secret, visible only to the sky and to those who brave the mountain. In 1963, a hoard of metal work was found on the slopes of Cadair Idris, not far from the Minffordd Path. It included artefacts that date back to the Iron Age, and a piece of Roman bronze. The origins and purpose of the hoard is debated, but one explanation suggests that the waters of Llyn Cau lake could have been the focus, perhaps visited for ritual purposes – this llyn is thought to have been a place of sacred importance in the Iron Age.

Now, the Minffordd Path begins with slate steps that pass through an ancient 'relict' oak wood. The oaks line a narrow crevice in the mountainside through which a waterfall splashes in full flow, a spray of droplets clouding the air. Tree trunks and branches are cushioned with moss, and ferns sprout from their hollows – fronds light in the wind. We are walking through a Celtic rainforest – extremely rare habitats found only close to the sea, where conditions are right. They are believed to be under greater threat even than tropical rainforests. Like Wistman's Wood, this fragment is one of the lost rainforests of Britain. Once again, my fog chase has unexpectedly led me into temperate rainforest, and I find myself bewitched by the timeless power of old trees, entangled by tendrils of beard lichen.

Epiphytes, including lichens, absorb water directly from the air, so noting which types of lichens are visible, and where they grow, can give insights into the microclimate of a place, including its incidence of fog. The presence of lichen indicates a moist environment (this is also true of moss). Fog is a source of the moisture lichens need, and, absorbing it, they swell as they dampen. Tristan Gooley writes in *The Secret World of Weather* that 'lichens make a fog map' – lichen, he explains, can be used as a predictor of fog, even so far as indicating whether the fog comes at night or in the day (which lichens prefer because they, like us, tend to rest at night). When I began my journey I had not considered that rainforests might lie in my path, but rainforests thrive in the damp, and fog is an elemental mixture of air and water, so it makes sense that locations where rainforests exist have a tendency to fog. Here in this ancient rainforest – as in Wistman's Wood – the spiralling trees and vaporous air create an aura of untamed strangeness, of place as portal. Many of these rainforests have been rediscovered, and here in Eryri they are now being restored and protected by the Celtic Rainforests Wales project. Nevertheless, their future remains far from certain; wider public awareness and political pressure will be needed if we are to save our lost rainforests.

We keep the rushing water to our right as we climb, and slate steps give way to rocky trackway. Along its margins I notice white quartz shards, like those I found on Dartmoor. I pocket a couple and then follow their trail – sharp-edged, glowing waymarkers of the path. As we travel higher, the track becomes a winterbourne: one of those ephemeral streams that flow chiefly in winter, and only in the aftermath of rain. Water hurries down the mountainside – finding, as it must, the fastest way – and as the sun fights out from behind the clouds, the dark rock of the route ahead of us glints. We stop briefly where a wide drystone wall intersects the path with a small gate and sit on a boulder to hungrily munch Welsh cakes. I look back, down to the vivid fields of the valley below, where miniature cars follow the road home that winds around the base of the opposite hillside. The trees stand fragile against flattened bracken, and above them the clouds churn.

The landscape is stunning, but its magnitude is disquieting. Yet again I experience a tingle of connection – the sensation of stepping out of time for an instant. Susan Cooper's narratives of slipping from the present to the past feel more plausible up here, so close to the sky. It is through place, Cooper writes, that she creates her narratives that flicker in and out of time. Cadair Idris is a place where time does seem to flicker, and time itself is a sphere in which it is highly possible, indeed inevitable, to get lost:

an endless flow of moments and people become lost to time, lost to history. The ongoing process of retelling and sharing is what prevents folklore's stories from being lost to the past, and to find these stories of the mountain is also to find a depth of meaning and magic in weather that has, in many places, already been lost. The resonance of fog in local folklore shows how layers of significance can enrich a place. This mountain, and the landscape that surrounds it, are abundant in stories. With the Brenin Llwyd in mind, I think how it might feel to become lost here – the alarming shift that would occur if a sudden fog did fall and the rocky route (that now seems so obvious) was suddenly rendered invisible. We would be navigating blind, with little more than the sound of the water as our guide.

During the final part of our climb, trees and bracken fall away, leaving only grass and scattered rocks to either side. We do lose the path for a little while, and squelch through boggy ground where there are unexpectedly deep holes to avoid. Following Dan up a long flight of stepped stone towards some boulders, I begin to wonder whether we might have lost our way altogether, but as we reach the top I see Llyn Cau below me – its waters lustrous black. The lake is said to be bottomless – the haunt of an *afanc* (a mythological lake monster sometimes described as a Welsh water dragon). I see wind stirring the surface of the llyn, and hear the frenzied crashing of several thin streams rushing down the mountain to meet the lake. I inhale the unsullied scent of water, lichen and sky. Behind the lake is the sweeping spread of the mountain with its distinctive ridge, where two small silhouettes move along the top towards the summit.

I make up my mind to swim while the heat of the climb

clings to me, and before I lose my nerve. Besides – I reason, stripping down to my costume – how many chances will I get to swim in the home of a water dragon? I clamber tentatively around the rocks on the lake edge, splash a little of the clear water on my arms and stretch out into the lake to swim. The water's frigid force clutches at my chest and I count my strokes, but before my breathing regulates, I realise I'm out of my depth, feeling small and suddenly fearful of becoming lost to this bottomless pool. It's the most glacial water I have ever felt. I turn, swim back quickly and climb out. My fingers are stiff with cold and I fumble to dress, but afterwards, warming my hands and sipping hot chocolate, a buzz spreads though my limbs and I'm completely exhilarated. I look up towards the mountain summit and see that drifting cloud has materialised at the top – in the court of the Brenin Llwyd there is mist, moving fast.

High in the air near the peak, two ravens wheel gracefully, massive black wings outstretched. Ravens are connected to another Welsh king, Bendigeidfran or Brân, whose name means 'raven' or 'crow'. They are birds that pair for life, and for a while my love and I stand together watching them. There is another way of getting lost – a conscious way which involves choosing to lose yourself to a place or experience. Rebecca Solnit calls this voluntary surrender 'a psychic state achievable through geography'. Looking up at the ravens, I briefly experience it: I lose myself to the mountain, to the moment, to the man who stands beside me, to a place that is not within my control. This way of getting lost can also represent a kind of surrender to the unknown – Keats' 'negative capability' – a willingness to accept uncertainty and mystery. In getting lost like this you may come to find another, different way, and unexpectedly I do feel changed by my time on the mountain, as if I have rediscovered a braver, more open part of myself that in the difficult pandemic years had become forgotten or lost. I take a kind of joy in surrendering to this mountain that has shown itself to be far beyond my imaginings of it, a place that knows the stillness of forever. But the moment is brief – the weather is volatile, the wind grows stronger, and my fingers have once again become numb.

Along the side of the mountain, a line of sheep crosses, stepping from rock to rock, and above them foggy cloud drifts across the summit. A whisper of dark stories is in the wind, and for the first time on my fog-chasing journey, I wish not to find fog – I hope that the Brenin Llwyd's twisting tendrils will not grow and multiply to follow us down the mountainside. As we turn around and make our way back, I notice narrow tracks crossing through the grass that I hadn't observed as we came up: sheep paths, or perhaps desire lines – unplanned, often-walked paths that (like water) tend to find the fastest way. Down beside the river, near the base of the Minffordd Path, we pass a twisted hazel tree, chalky with lichen. A tangled clump of sheep's wool clings to its bottom branch.

In mountainous areas, fog can equate to death. The story of a hungering king who conceals himself within (and perhaps directs) the fog is a folkloric representation of the horror of becoming lost, not just in the fog, but to the fog – to death – and of never returning from the mountain. Folklore can be a way of transmitting knowledge, or truth that might otherwise be lost or ignored. The fear of being snatched by the Brenin

Llwyd would have been an effective deterrent, and so, in this way, his stories kept people safe.

Another folkloric figure associated with both death and mist is Gwrach-y-Rhibyn, or Hag of the Mist. Found in fog, but rarely – if ever – seen, this hag manifested as a haggard, ugly old woman whose presence foreshadowed death. If, one dreadful night, you should hear the Hag of the Mist call your name you knew that death would soon come for you. She was similar to another spectral figure known as a Cyhyraeth whose disembodied lamentation was a sign of imminent doom. The Hag of the Mist was also associated with streams – which on Cadair Idris are plentiful. Fog can spark our horror of the un-known – like the dark, it was thought to conceal the unreal, grim or ghostly – and yet the hags who resided in the mist offered nothing physical to fear, only awful intuition and the sound of their voices. The fog held and concealed these por-tentous, mist-shrouded female spirits who appear to offer an older, bleaker counterpoint to the fog-self that I seek. But in her book *Hagitude*, Sharon Blackie looks to reclaim the hag, writing that women can find meaning in the second half of their lives through fulfilling a personal calling and releasing their 'unique Inner Hag'. Perhaps a fog-self is a kind of nascent inner hag – an emergent creative spirit set loose by the mist, a splinter of self to be coaxed out into the light.

In 'Y Niwl' ('The Mist'), a poem by fourteenth-century Welsh poet Dafydd ap Gwilym, mist is portrayed as a cloying force that detains the poem's protagonist, who is on the way to meet a girl. In the poem's English translation (by Swansea University and the University of Wales), he compares the mist to draping textiles: 'an endless blanket in the sky / a grey cowl making the ground one colour'. As the imagery in the poem builds layers of comparisons, the fabric of the mist becomes increasingly heavy and ominous: from a 'shaggy cloak of the lands' to a 'broad web of thick deceptive cambric'. Dafydd ap Gwilym associates this mutable mist with the same wild huntsman Gwyn ap Nudd and the magic fair folk: 'Gwyn's tribe'. The mist spreads and shifts state to a 'speckled smoke which gets everywhere' – it is inescapable. The protagonist's romantic tryst is thwarted by this dense, obstructive mist that fails to dissipate: neither moon nor stars can penetrate – it remains 'forever black and confining'. This mist seems almost sentient: it 'wets stealthily' and blocks the speaker's path – if mist is a character here, it feels like a malicious one. In the poem, as in the folkloric stories, mist and fog are given agency and may have been created – or controlled – by the otherworldly. More than just a weather condition, fog can represent a threatening, potentially malignant entity to be treated with wariness, respect and even fear.

In a vast, untamed place, respect is an appropriate response – to fog, and to the mountain itself. Both landscape and weatherscape here are mighty – earth and sky are intertwined – and although the form of the mountain is unchanging, the weather interacts fluidly with its various spaces. Wind ripples the lake, clouds cling to the peak, snow – which falls heavily the week after our climb – covers slopes with a sparkling mantle. This wild place is neither benign nor malignant, but it is unpredictable, and choosing to step onto a mountain means relinquishing an element of control.

In my experience, the same can be true of choosing to walk in the fog: even the most familiar locations become disorientating. I recall a recent foggy morning when I set off walking in the woods near my home. Making my way along a narrow path through the trees, a sense of unease suddenly crept over me: I felt spun around and confused; I was inexplicably lost. The fog was thick, the trees were uniform, and the path was not the waymarked track I expected: I had strayed onto a desire line. I froze on the spot, unsure whether to turn back and try to retrace my steps, or to forge ahead in hope of finding a landmark I recognised. I tried to summon the shape of the woods into my mind but had lost any sense of which way was home. I had no choice but to follow my feet, staying firmly on the narrow line through the trees, trusting in instinct to find my way back. Despite being within walking distance of my house, I felt panicked – losing myself *to* the fog is a pleasure but losing myself *in* the fog felt alarming. After what seemed like an age, I began to notice a subtle change in the light, a brightening on the horizon – drawing closer, I found I was approaching the edge of the wood where it joined a field – the muddy route that ran parallel was my way home.

Aberdyfi, where we stop for a restorative drink in a snug seafront pub on our way back from the mountain, hosts a piece of underwater art called 'The Time & Tide Bell'. It celebrates a legend which tells of a lost and sunken land – the kingdom of Cantre'r Gwaelod, said to have existed around 5,000 years ago until (the story tells) it became lost to the sea, immersed by the waters of Cardigan Bay when the floodgates that protected it were accidentally left open, submerging both land and people. 'The Time & Tide Bell', created as part of a project by sculptor Marcus Vergette, hangs suspended beneath the pier's wooden jetty and it is rung by the movement of the sea at high tide each day. Thanks to the particular chemistry of the Dyfi estuary, the bronze bell has turned a vibrant shade of aquamarine blue. Its pitch varies according to how deeply it is submerged in the water, and it has been designed to serve as a long-time marker of sea levels, with the frequency of its ringing increasing as sea levels rise – this bell tolls as an auditory indication of climate change.

Cantre'r Gwaelod was said to have incorporated an ancient forest, now lost with the kingdom beneath the waves. When Storm Hannah battered the coastline in 2019, swathes of petrified stumps appeared: the remains of peat-covered trees. Some linked these trees to the lost land of Cantre'r Gwaelod, and archaeologists consider that there would have been life in this once-submerged forest as far back as the Bronze Age. The extreme weather of climate change may have revealed here what long ago was lost, but the threat of rising sea levels and coastal erosion means that there is so much more to lose. On the day we visit Aberdyfi, the tide is low and the bell is silent, but later I listen to a sound recording of another of Vergette's Time & Tide bells: the chime echoes and reverberates, mournfully fading and then gradually rising – vibrations blending with the splashing of the sea. As we drive home, away from mountain and coast, I notice the flash of a rainbow in the rearview mirror and I watch it fade into the hills.

A few weeks after our walk on Cadair Idris, on Valentine's Day, I spend a frustrating morning unsuccessfully chasing fog. My new weather-forecasting app has offered me a 50 per cent chance of fog in Bristol, and I've seen photographs taken on recent mornings of fog flowing under the Bristol Suspension

Bridge – a place of which I am extremely fond, having once lived for a year in a basement flat on a road nearby – so after I drop my youngest son at school, I decide to take a chance. All the way to Bristol it is foggy, but as I turn off the motorway it begins to fade and brighten, and I arrive to find the bridge and the Avon Gorge river valley bathed in sunshine. Opting to stay and work in a cafe for an hour, I find myself passing the end of the road where I lived.

One dusky evening twenty years ago, as I was walking home with Dan, piano music floated out into the summer air from the open sash windows of the tall Georgian house on this corner – the aching strains of Beethoven's *Moonlight Sonata*. We stopped to listen, hand in hand. Today the corner is quiet, and opposite the cafe at the bottom of the hill, the proprietor of a vintage shop is lining up her merchandise on the pavement. She wears a brown fur coat, like the ones that hang in her shop doorway. On a Formica table is a box filled with old postcards, two for a pound. I rummage absent-mindedly through scenes of holiday destinations, old buildings and cloudy steam railways. As I turn to walk away, something makes me stop to dig a little deeper. 'Valentine's Post Card' reads the back of a card. '1d stamp if with only sender's name and address and 5 words conventional greeting'. I flip it over, and there between my fingers I find a black and white postcard of Cadair Idris, taken from Penygareg. Beneath it is a postcard of a second scene: Corris and Cadair Idris – also in black and white with thick foggy cloud covering the top of the mountain. I have found fog here after all. The backs of the postcards are blank, but I feel as if I've received a message.

4

THE HAUNTED IN-BETWEEN –
EAST ANGLIAN FENS

(roke – steam fog – sense of touch)

Fog is weather that becomes a space – somewhere that is neither here nor there, a temporary fissure. To me, fog seems to open up a rift in reality: I step out of everyday time and into a cool quietness – a locus of latent magic. But there is one particular foggy place in which the landscape itself exists as a liminal place that is simultaneously land and water. It is a region that connects countryside and sea, where the boundaries between earth and sky become hazy and blurred, and the topography of the past haunts the people of the present: the East Anglian Fens. This is another familiar landscape to me: when I was in primary school, a change of job for my father led us to relocate from Devon to East Anglia, moving hundreds of miles from the house by the castle in Okehampton to a cottage in a Suffolk village and later – in my early teens – to a town just beyond Fenland borders called Bury-St-Edmunds. There, I lived under that same endless, painterly sky that fades to a flat horizon and, while I don't remember how I first heard the stories, I grew up knowing, as if they had seeped beneath my skin, old tales of the foggy Fens, inhabited by boggarts and will-o'-the-wisps and haunted by the cold touch of ghosts. Although they were not far away, the Fens – a haunted land, a marshy in-between – seemed completely other to my own comfortable hometown.

Fenland borders have long been, like the Fens themselves, liquid and ever-changing, but today the Fens make up around one million acres on the east coast of England, inland from England's largest bay – the Wash (a stretch of coastline where I spent more than one childhood summer holiday under canvas). Once, the Fens were untamed wetlands connected by a complex, changeable network of rivers, creeks and lakes (known locally as meres). Bent willow trees and whispering reed beds grew in the endless marshes, still water reflecting drifting cloud patterns of never-ending skies. Fog lay low over these wetlands, rising from the water at dusk in 'shifting wreaths' (steam fog, caused by water vapour condensing as it met the cool evening air). Here in the east of England, fog – rising evening fog in particular – is known locally as 'roke'. The Fens have often been characterised as foggy, dark and brooding, and to outsiders this complex landscape appeared inaccessible and treacherous.

To the Fen people, who understood and respected their environment, it was a rich habitat that provided a wealth of resources. They made their homes and gardens on areas of high ground and raised cattle on seasonally dry grasslands. They skillfully navigated the waterways that intersected the marshes, harvesting food – fish, eels and waterbirds – as well as building materials, such as reed for thatching. The Fens offered their inhabitants a unique and bountiful domain – an intricate watery world. But others saw the Fens as valuable land that could be utilised for agriculture – as far back as Roman times there were attempts to drain the wetlands, and in some parishes, active drainage had been underway from Saxon times. King Charles I carried out the co-ordinated drainage that had been suggested by his father King James I, following disastrous floods in 1603. In 1631, a wide-scale plan for drainage was proposed and funded by the Earl of Bedford, in association with a group of speculators known as the 'Adventurers', and a Dutch wetland engineer called Cornelius Vermuyden was employed to oversee the work. The enforced drainage projects were deeply unpopular with Fen dwellers, who lost their common land without compensation and they responded to perceived attacks on their environment with repeated uprisings – resistance and sabotage led by a group called the Fen Tigers. But drainage went ahead – by its piece-meal nature fragmenting the Fens – and the interconnected wetlands were forever changed. It is difficult now to conceive of the extent of that lost, foggy waterscape.

In my hometown near the Fenland edge, I was at a thresh-old – living in those strange years of yearning and learning that fall between childhood and adulthood. I was preoccupied by the moon; perhaps all teenage girls are? I wore blue dun-garees printed with crescent moons and a tiny moon hung around my neck on a leather thread. Sleeping in a tent in my best friend's garden the summer after our GSCE exams, we saw the crescent moon rise – it was a time of wishing. On nights when the moon was full, I watched its gentle glow spread across the wooden floorboards of my bedroom at the top of the tall, narrow house. Reaching out my hand, I touched silvery light with my fingertips, and felt the pulse of possibility. I looked on the moon with love. Fen people, too, were once known for their love of the moon. At night – or in a fog – the Fens were dangerous. If you could not see clearly, it was easy to lose your way and slip from the path into marsh or mere. You might easily drown, grasping in vain for a branch to catch hold of. Moonlight was protective and lifesaving and accordingly the moon held a high status in Fenland folklore. The folktale I remembered best (one with the power to make me shiver if I recalled it while walking home in the dark) was the tale of the Dead Moon.

The beautiful moon – so the story went – shone over the Fens, keeping the people safe night after night. On cloudy or foggy nights (when her light could not be seen) boggarts, witches, will-o'-the-wisps and slimy dead things that lived in the dark pools could come out and roam the marshland. The sweet moon, hearing of this, stepped down from the sky, covering her glowing hair with a long, dark cloak, and she walked bravely out into the marshes to see what was amiss. But she slipped and was caught on a snag (a standing dead tree, like an arboreal ghost). Gripped by the slippery touch of evil creatures, the frightened moon found herself trapped under a heavy stone, her pure light extinguished. With the moon gone, the people endured night after night of horror-filled darkness until eventually some of them ventured into the marsh to find and rescue her. As they heaved away the stone that bound her, a blinding white light flashed and rose up, and the moon reappeared, brighter than ever, in the sky. While it isn't witches or boggarts that a teenage girl fears as she walks home alone through evening streets, hood up and head down, gripping a door key between her knuckles like a charm, to me (as to the Fen people) fog or darkness was heavy with menace and the moon offered both illumination and talismanic power.

One Fenland ghost story illustrates the dangers of venturing across a fen on a moonless, foggy night. On an evening around 300 years ago, so local legend tells, a 'fen slodger' (wildfowler) called Joseph Hempsall set off across Wicken Fen (then known as Big Bog) to drink with his friends in a tavern. A thick, and by some accounts unearthly, fog descended, plunging the fen into impenetrable gloom, and at the end of the evening his friends begged him not to make the journey home, but to stay the night in the tavern. Joseph Hempsall demurred and strode off into the fog. He was never seen alive again.

A few days later, when his friends went to his house in search of him, they encountered a blanched shadow of the man he had been. It said to them: 'As I am now, so one day will ye be. Fetch me from Big Bog and bury me in Wicken Churchyard', before vanishing. On the fen bank, they found Joseph Hempsall's body semi-submerged in fen water, a terrified expression frozen on his face. Some say his ghost haunts the area on foggy nights, uttering the same bleak warning: 'As I am now, so one day will ye be.' No one ever knew what happened to Hempsall in the fog – perhaps he encountered the Lantern Men (atmospheric ghost lights sometimes seen on Wicken Fen and believed to be evil spirits that would lure the unsuspecting to a watery death), or perhaps he succumbed to the fog's disorientating and relentless touch. Whatever took place, he became a creature in between – not fully present nor truly absent, neither alive nor dead.

When I return to East Anglia in search of fog, Wicken Fen is the first fen I visit. It is late afternoon and I am just twenty miles away from the town in which I spent my teenage years. I have not been back there for over a decade and it feels at once tantalisingly near and impossibly distant. I have come to Wicken Fen because it is a small surviving fragment of untouched wetland, described by the National Trust as 'a window onto a lost East Anglian landscape'. Having never been drained, it has retained its deep peat bogs and serves as a living reminder of what the Fens once were – a gateway between past and present, an unsteady mingling of water and land.

I arrive in the fading light: reeds blow in the wind and crepuscular rays slice the sky, pointing down towards what looks like a black wooden windmill at the edge of the fen, its sails frozen. This is a wind pump, once used to drain turf pits for peat digging. But here, deep below old, undrained Sedge Fen (at the heart of Wicken Fen) are rare and precious layers of millennia-old untouched peat. The fen has a distinctive smell: a shade mossy, a touch musty, a whiff of decomposing plant matter. I cross marshy ground on a wooden boardwalk as a roe deer skitters along the edges. Light and darkness intersect here in this low, watery landscape; the marsh's peaty depths are bottomless and black, reflecting the sky up to me. This unsettling dark mirror is what I remember of the Fens. On the water's surface where dead leaves float is an evanescent dance of sunshine and waterlight, a twinkling between the reeds. Twilight – the in-between time – is fast approaching. I watch echoes of clouds drift across the water; on a moonlit night, the full moon reflected in these pools might well appear to be trapped in the watery dark.

To avoid the gruesome creatures they believed to inhabit the marshes, superstitious Fen-dwellers typically avoided the fog and tried not to go out alone in the dark. As protection, they would carry charms known as safe-keeps clutched tight in their fingers or secreted away. Another folktale tells of Long Tom: a man who considered himself too brave to require a safe-keep and mockingly determined to cross the marsh alone one night with only a lantern to guide him. Beside a willow-snag he was beset by nameless, swarming horrors and felt the clammy, grasping touch of a dead, disembodied hand. It pulled him into the marsh, where he was devoured by blackness.

Superstition, and belief in witchcraft, was long prevalent here, and in the 'Fens & Folklore' room at the top of the Museum of Cambridge, I find a small collection of charms known as 'witch bottles' – slender, clear glass bottles tarnished with the remnants of the protective elements (alcohol, hair, nail clippings and even urine) that they once contained. One, which visibly holds pieces of silk and wool, has plant strands worked into the glass itself. These bottles tended to be found buried under fireplaces or floorboards or plastered inside walls. They are emblematic of a period of time when (following a succession of English Witchcraft Acts passed in the sixteenth and seventeenth centuries) a woman – particularly if she was in some way unusual or marginalised – could find herself accused of witchcraft on the most nebulous of grounds. Several witch trials took place in Ely, at the heart of the Fens, and Matthew Hopkins, the ominously named Witchfinder General, fa-mously held a series of witch trials in Bury-St-Edmunds, resulting in a string of executions. As a young woman, standing beside my window watching moonlight illuminate the town, I was as yet unaware of that grim chapter in its history. Now, in the museum, I marvel over a blue glass orb – a witch ball – made to be hung in a house window. By reflecting the light, it was intended to dazzle witches, deterring them from approaching the home. Despite its age, it is unnervingly flawless, reminding me of a full, blue moon; I feel an oddly strong urge to reach out and stroke its mesmerising surface but it is separate from me, contained in the cabinet.

As the perceived haunt of evil or supernatural beings, fog in the Fens represented danger, uncertainty and the threat of bad magic. In *Between Sunset and Moonrise* – R. H. Malden's ghost story set in the Fens – the protagonist walks home at night along a drove (a wide grass track that crosses a fen, sometimes edged by dykes). A thick white fog rolls quickly in, obscuring the stars and any hope of an emergent moon, and it appears to take on a life of its own. The fog splits and rolls back, so that the sides of the drove become 'two solid banks of white, with a narrow passage clear between them'. Into this fog-encircled space advances a dark and sinister collection of figures that merge into a gigantic shadow, a malignant Brocken Spectre: 'The mist closed behind him, so that his dark figure was thrown up against a solid background of white: much as mountain climbers are said sometimes to see their own shadows upon a bank of cloud.' In this story, fog not only blocks the light of the moon and stars, it turns the drove into an unholy tunnel – a dark passageway that harbours an overpowering force of murderous evil, as the fog manifests corporeally. Similarly, evening mist – roke – was sometimes considered to be the spectral forms of mist-wraiths, rising up from the water.

In 1901, author William Alfred Dutt described visiting a riverside inn on the 'mist-mantled marshes' of the nearby Norfolk Broads to speak to the rivermen of a time when 'the roke was dense as to hide even the windmills on the river-banks [...] of the marsh-fires which used to flicker over the festering swamps; and of the mist wraiths and phantom fisher-men of the meres and marshes'. Drawn to the mist-wraiths, I wonder if they originated from underwater – a kind of cloudy mermaid – or if they had once been human? Perhaps, living in a mist-mantled place, they had gradually absorbed so much mist that they eventually became it. Not for the first time, I feel that if I continue to chase fog, something similar could one day happen to me. Is a mist-wraith just a woman who has become more fog than self?

I visit Lakenheath Fen, an RSPB reserve, to walk along a drove. Mercifully, no fog tunnel appears – the sky is clear. To my left, the Little Ouse; to my right, a whispering reed bed and, behind it, a boggy poplar wood. This fen has been reclaimed, bought as arable farmland in 1995 – at which time I was in school nearby – and converted into a nature reserve. Originally a tract of Fenland marsh, it was returned to wa-terscape through the addition of a complex infrastructure and over 300,000 reeds, planted by volunteers. It's now home to a wealth of wildlife including otters, marsh harriers and bit-terns – the latter a secretive, thickset heron once so common here they were called 'fenman's turkey', but now endangered due to their need for reed bed habitat.

The road to the fen is bordered by expansive arable land – spreading black fields, their peaty soil edged by dykes. A pair of swans stand, white against ebony on the corner of a field. Here at Lakenheath Fen the earth below my feet is also dark, dark black, and it is noticeably springy. A quivering cry trembles out of the poplar wood. I can't identify the bird – the sound moves from tree to tree. Standing beside the water now, I look out across a silver mere and dip my hand into reeds – they are feathery, and gossamer-soft to touch. A couple of ducks swim off, disappearing along a tiny pathway through the reed bed, which stretches back to the horizon. I try to imagine away the surrounding fields, conjuring instead a vision of endless watery inlets and grassy islands. A walkway with a viewing platform stretches over the water and I step out onto it – a floating space in this area of resurrected wild. Later, I will hear on a podcast a sound-recording of the underwater soundscape of Strumpshaw Fen recorded with hydrophones. As a child, I regularly pond-dipped for water boatmen, and here, for the first time, I hear their cricket-like chatter. There is flowing and dripping of water and the soft sound of aquatic plants releasing bubbles of oxygen. Above the surface, the occasional bird call is audible. I listen over and over – it gives me a sense of submersion, as if I were plunging down below the black glass surface of the fen like a returning mist-wraith, feeling the sleek touch of peaty water glide across my skin.

I see actual mist only once on my visit to the Fens: as I approach the city of Ely, an insistent, misty drizzle softens the level landscape. From this hazy base, Ely Cathedral tower rises up. I have seen recent photographs of the cathedral enveloped in a thick fog, floating like an island in a cloudy ocean, and these dramatic scenes are what I had hoped for, but instead I receive light mizzle. Once, Ely was an actual island – the largest in the Fens. Its name means 'eel-district' or, in some interpretations, 'eel-island'. Eels were a highly prized food source that was plentiful in the Fens, with some taxes in this area at one time payable in eels, including to Bury-St-Edmunds Abbey, which collected eel rent from the commoners. The now-ruined abbey and its grounds were a regular haunt of mine in my teens – then, lying on a sunny bank I listened to mix tapes on my Walkman. My best friend and I tiptoed across the crumbling abbey walls together and ate our sandwiches in the rose garden.

Now, in Ely, I am walking part of the Eel Trail along the River Ouse. Eels, I read on an information board, live and feed in the river for around ten years and then, on a dark and moonless night, they will set off on a 3,000-mile journey to breed in the Sargasso Sea. The thought of the slimy touch of an eel has always made me recoil slightly, but I am struck now by their tenacity. As Fen people remained safely at home on a dark or foggy night, below the river surface eels were embarking on a long and dangerous passage. Later, in the local museums I will see willow-woven eel grigs (baited traps used to catch eels), and the rather more brutal eel gleeves (sharp, fork-like spears used to pin them). On the far side of the river, I notice a small marina with motorboats of the sort I remember from being taken out onto the Norfolk Broads as a child. Light splinters the surface and a pair of swans glide by. The sunshine touches a narrowboat moored on the opposite bank – the boat's name, I read (as if it were a sign), is *Misty*.

In the environs of Ely there are unsettling presences with

watery associations, seen only in the mist. It is said that on misty evenings a phantom barge appears, crewed by ghostly monks chanting hymns. Some say the barge is transporting the shrouded corpse of a woman, suggested to be St Withburga, whose body was supposedly stolen by the Abbot of Ely. Accounts vary as to whether this barge haunts the River Great Ouse or its tributary the Little Ouse. Ghost sightings are difficult to research: the internet, like the river, is vague and misty, swirling with varying and unevidenced rumours. At the confluence of the Great Ouse and the Little Ouse, another group of ghosts have been seen on foggy nights near to the village of Southery, at Brandon Creek. These stories centre on a waterside pub called the Ship Inn, which is told to have been the location first of murders, and then, in retribution, brutal executions of the murderers that took place in the river itself. The dead men are believed to return in the dark and the fog to haunt the place where they met their end.

I decide to brave a stop at this pub, and it rises up suddenly ahead of me from a spreading, featureless landscape, sitting on a promontory beside a bridge at an intersection where rivers and counties meet. This is a stopping place, a halfway point – somewhere in-between. Standing beside the river in the pub garden, I sense an emptiness that may be nothing more than the loneliness of heavy grey clouds touching endless horizon, but on a foggy night this would doubtless seem a spooky, isolated spot. A plume of smoke curls up into the distance, and its familiar acrid smell pulls me into the past, when the wind blew across my hometown from the sugar beet factory and I kept my sash window tightly closed. Inside the pub, it is warm and friendly – nothing hints at a dark past or a ghostly presence other than the beer on tap, which is Adnam's Ghost Ship. As I drive away, road parallel to river, the sun is low in the sky. Two walkers along the riverbank become momentarily silhouetted – huge and inhuman against the sun – looming large and shadowy like unnamed monsters rising from the fen. Shaken, I blink, and the illusion is gone.

A final folktale, the story of 'mist-whisperer' Tiddy Mun, recounts the draining of the Fens and the fading of the fog. Tiddy Mun was a strange creature, small as a child with long white hair and beard. He wore a pale-grey gown that blended with the evening mist, and he lived in the depths of the marsh waterholes. At the end of the day, as mist flowed over the marshes in waves, Tiddy Mun went walking. When he passed by, it was like the sound of running water or the drift of the wind. If waters rose too high, and their homes were at risk of flooding, Fen people would set off in the light of the new moon to call out over the marsh to 'Tiddy Mun without a name' for help. His answer – the cry of a peewit – meant he had heard their pleas, and the next day the waters would drop. When the marshes came to be drained, Tiddy Mun grew angry. As water disappeared into dykes, the drainage workers too began to disappear – into sunken graves. Soon the fen people themselves felt his displeasure: cows pined, pigs starved, ponies went lame and children took sick.

Believing themselves to be cursed, the people set out once again in the light of the new moon and stood at the edge of the dyke. Pouring in fresh water, they cried: 'Tiddy Mun without a name, here's water for you. Lift your curse!' Into the darkness rose a wailing sound, the cry of a newborn child, and mother after mother standing by the dyke felt the icy touch of her own dead baby's hand, the coldness of their departed lips kissing her cheek, the flutter of angelic wings. Here were their lost children, they cried, pleading with Tiddy Mun to break his spell and let their living children grow up healthy and strong. Suddenly, all fell still but for the water lapping at their feet. The call of a peewit echoed across the marsh, and they knew that the curse was lifted. After that, at every new moon, the people returned to the dyke with fresh water for Tiddy Mun, but although they strained their eyes, looking for a figure swathed in flowing fog, he was never seen again.

If this story passed me by as a teen, now that I am a mother its reference to the sudden felt sensation of your dead child's touch strikes deep – it is an unbearably disquieting image. Where did the lost children go? Perhaps they, like the mist-wraiths, floated up from the depths, disappearing into the air like sighs. Sometimes, beneath the invisible light of a new moon, a wind crossing the Fens may reach out like a caress in the darkness, but there is no longer copiously flowing water, and the peewit's cry will not be heard. Tiddy Mun, water-loving spirit of the Fens, faded away when the land was drained, and much of the fog – as well as some of the folklore – seems to have gone with him. Although fog comes to the Fens, it is now nowhere near as common – evening mist cannot rise up from the marshes if the marshes are no more.

Recurrent Fen fogs could be a weatherscape of the past but Tiddy Mun's distinctive cry may yet be heard again – 'peewit' describes the call of the lapwing, a species of bird that the RSPB is hoping to attract back to Lakenheath Fen with the upcoming creation of an area of grassland and wet sedge fen, adjacent to their current reserve: It could be that on my next visit, 'peewit' will be the birdsong I hear. Some small corners of wetland are gradually returning and this landscape of the in-between remains in flux. The reclamation of wet land to dry is in itself a continuous process and one day, alarmingly, flood waters may yet return to the Fens. Archaeologist Francis Pryor (a fen dweller) sees it as an inevitability that the drastic drop in land levels, which occurred when the Fens were drained, coupled with steadily rising sea levels will result in some degree of flooding in the Fens. The Fens are haunted both by what has happened here, and by what may be yet to come.

Pryor knows better than anyone the layers of the past that are buried beneath the Fens, preserved in the peat. One foggy morning in 1982, walking along a dykeside, he made a discovery half-buried in a heap of sludge that had been removed from the bottom of the drainage ditch as part of an archaeological dyke survey. To most people, it would have been nothing more than a discarded piece of wood, but Pryor saw something incredible. With his field of vision narrowed by the fog, did he see more clearly? Perhaps in the fog the past became visible. It may have been purely a fortuitous find on that particular murky morning, but what Pryor unearthed was an oak post that had been sharpened by a Bronze Age axe: he had discovered part of a one-kilometre-long man-made wooden causeway intersected by a gigantic platform around the size of a football stadium. The anaerobic conditions of the Fenland peat bog soil had preserved this astonishing monument for over 3,000 years. Just as incredible was the discovery of numerous metal objects that also dated back to the Bronze

Age. Around, or close to, the five rows of upright timbers joined by horizontal planks that formed the structure Pryor describes as a 'post alignment' they dug up swords, daggers, spearheads, brooches, pins, rings, bracelets and more.

This elaborately fashioned walkway was not merely an extensive wooden bridge construction to cross often-flooded, wet, boggy land – it also seems to have been a site of ongoing ritual significance. The precious items gathered around the posts had not been accidentally lost or discarded – they were likely to have been votive offerings to the waters during ceremonial rites. The Flag Fen Bronze Age post alignment was, as Annie Proulx points out in *Fen, Bog and Swamp*, a liminal space – a border between life and death. Many of the rites that took place there were probably funerary in nature – ceremonies for the disposal or remembrance of the dead, with the resultant offerings presumably intended to aid the deceased on their journey into an afterlife. Betrothals, marriages and apprenticeship initiations may also have occurred, and rites were probably held as small gatherings, with the post alignment possibly subdivided into smaller ceremonial 'rooms' that functioned as family shrines. Water is thought to have had ritual significance to Bronze Age people, and I can see how, looking down from the wooden trackway at a glassy surface reflecting their faces back to them, they might have considered the waters below the raised path as a kind of flickering boundary-line between the world of the living and – beneath the surface – the world of their ancestors. Objects and souls could pass down through the waterline to reach the next world. The structure of the trackway itself may even have been built as deliberately transitory and impermanent, its own eventual vanishment into the peaty depths a known inevitability.

A visit to Flag Fen is an act of imagination. I find it in an unprepossessing spot not far from Peterborough: industrial buildings on the skyline, rubbish littering a nearby field. But a wide-winged red kite hovers over a drainage ditch, the trees around the water-encircled stilted visitors' centre are loud with birdsong, and yet another pair of swans walk out towards the boundary fence. This is somewhere that offers a pathway to the past – an opportunity to journey back in time. I think of the treasures buried here in the mud and imagine the sensation of first discovering, on a foggy morning, some-thing incredible that has lain untouched for 3,000 years. I step into a room where timbers from the post alignment have been preserved, exactly where they were found. Mostly un-derwater, only the very tops of the posts emerge, misted from above at intervals by damp spray. A mural painted around the walls shows a representation of the Bronze Age landscape in each of the four seasons. The summer panel opposite shows lush green vegetation, with a blaze of yellow Flag Iris flowers (for which Flag Fen is named). Behind me, the winter panel has patches of reeds surrounded by spreading, looking-glass water. The panels to my left and right (spring and autumn) depict the post alignment as it would have looked. Cutting a path through marsh and flood meadow, running parallel to the main drove, are five intimidating rows of sharp upright posts (with a patchwork of timbers underneath), disappearing into the infinite distance. I experience a wave of awe at the thought of this monumental structure, wooden cathedral of the in-between, a crossing place between worlds. It stretches so far across the Fens, and so distantly back into time.

The Flag Fen Archaeology Park has no foundations – it floats on water above the archaeological remains below. Crossing the bridge, I walk over, and into, the past. Suspended above the fen, the museum is an ever-moving space within which are held artefacts discovered along the causeway – swords, rings and brooches. They are contained in glass cabinets, too fragile to withstand touch. But by their very existence, the dead reach out their hands, as if to grasp the living – they draw me in, fascinated, beckoning me towards strange mysteries. My head whirls with the incomprehensible twisting of time. On my way back to the car, I duck into a reconstruction Bronze Age roundhouse. Inside it is gloomy; I smell residual ash from a fire and feel the wind blowing under the roof. I shut my eyes – trying to traverse time, if only for an instant – but remain firmly inside my own head, in the twenty-first century. Stepping outside, I notice tiny white flowers growing in among the earth and moss atop the roundhouse's thatched roof. I run my fingers over its edges. Moss is bouncy to the touch but the reed, full of mud, is brittle and crumbles beneath my fingers. And then, at last, I am transported back to the past – not to the Bronze Age but to childhood – for once, I was a thatcher's daughter. My father knows how to weave straw and reed – not into gold, but into a roof, which I always considered just as magical. I would visit him perched high up on the ridge as I stood below in my iris-yellow raincoat, looking up at my daddy who could touch the sky.

Sedge, used by thatchers for ridges, was once a valuable crop grown in the Fens. Written records from as far back as

1419 show Great Fen saw-sedge being harvested at Wicken Fen, and it is cut by the rangers today. On my visit to Wicken Fen, the sedge swishes, but I keep my fingers away: I know it can be razor sharp to touch. When he was thatching, my dad's hands were rarely without cuts. Before leaving, I duck into the Wicken Fen bird hide because sundown is the time that hen harriers come in to roost. I gaze out across a flat expanse of reed bed, the light fading from gold to blue – this is the transition from day to night and the birds come to the space between. The reeds flash in the path of the retreating sun.

Next to me a birdwatcher with binoculars spots a harrier, way in the distance. I wait, my hands becoming numb. Light leaches from the landscape and the clouds turn pink. On the horizon, beside a row of trees, I make out the tiny speck of a harrier flying towards us, but it disappears again, and I can't be sure it was ever there at all. The sun is visibly sinking now – a puddle of molten fire falling below the horizon. The flames drip away, but a harrier does not come. If there's one thing I have learned here, it's to not cross the Fens after dark, so I leave the hide while the dykes yet shine. High above the fen, flanked by vapour trails, a slither of moon grows slowly brighter. I look up at it with love and gratitude. *Guide me home*, I think. Suddenly, I am startled by the ethereal silhouette of a barn owl flying up from the reeds and across the path. It swoops on wan wings out of the gathering night, like a silent and graceful ghost, haunting the Fenland in-between. Turning its head momentarily towards me, it is gone, enveloped into the fen.

The evening roke has not once risen up from the Fens during my visit, and I wonder to what extent the 'fen-sucked fogs' that Shakespeare references in *King Lear* disappeared when the Fens were drained. Fog was an important element of the lost Fenland landscape – a physical incarnation of the spirit of the Fens, like a manifestation of the genius loci. What I am chasing now may be but the spectre of it. In my mind, I try to conjure the sensation of fog's cool touch, recalling a foggy day in my local woods. Water dripped from the trees onto my head and, one by one, crisp beech leaves drifted and twisted slowly down through the silver air. The fog was chill against my skin and in my lungs. It was a sensation not unlike winter swimming: the encompassing cold, the intake of breath, a sharpening of focus and a total submersion in the moment. I chase fog because it preoccupies me – it compels me – but also because I carry it with me. Wherever I go, it sings beneath my skin.

On the last day of my Fens trip, in an alleyway so tiny that its entrance is easily missed, I discover the Haunted Bookshop. I had passed by here many times in my youth but I never stopped to look, let alone venture into the alley's gloomy depths. Unlike the pub, this place advertises its ghosts, and the bookshop is haunted, the bookseller tells me when I ask, both by a young, fair-haired woman in a long white gown, and occasionally by the drifting scent of violets. For many moons, a fair-haired girl has haunted me too – not as a ghost, but as a treasured memory: my best friend, blonde as I am dark, died at the age of eighteen. She had slender, tapered fingers and tucked her hair behind her ear when she was thinking. We wrote each other letters every day, even if we knew we would be together from dawn until dusk, and I loved her in the wild, intense way that teenage girls love their one true friend. I rarely return to the town in which we grew up because those streets, for me, are too full of shades of who we once were. I think of us in our dungarees, walking with arms linked, and although I try to recall the cool touch of her hand on my wrist, the memory has been blurred by the fog of time. Now, in the Fenland bookshop, I inhale deeply, hoping for violets, but all I can smell is the musty vanillin of old books. On a shelf by the window, I find a hardback copy of *Towers in the Mist* by Elizabeth Goudge, and I carry it away in a paper bag.

5

The Fog Horn – Devon and Cornwall Coast

(haag – sea fog – sense of sound)

The lighthouse clings to the tip of a lonely headland, far beyond the end of the road and reached only by a winding primrose path. I follow this path out along the clifftop: to my right, a grassy bank smothered in sunny flowers; to my left a wavy stone wall and, below it, more patches of primroses. They tumble all the way down to the turquoise sea, which eddies gently. Ahead of me, Start Point Lighthouse disappears and reappears as I turn each corner. It is Gothic in style – a smooth tower with a few small windows and a battlemented parapet, above which are the diamond-shaped panes of glass that form the Lantern Room, a gold wind-vane perched on its roof. Two square white houses with matching green doors and windowsills cluster close to the lighthouse base, enclosed by another low wall. A swathe of delicate, bell-like flowers – chalky-pale, like lighthouse paint – grow right up to its stones. These are Allium triquetrum or, less elegantly, three-cornered leek. A large vivid yellow sign hangs on the metal gate. 'Warning,' it reads, 'Fog Signal – the public are advised that a fog signal emitting a very loud noise may be sounded in this vicinity at any time without prior warning.' My heart skips a little and I turn to examine the horizon in vain hope of approaching fog, wishing that the spring sky was not such a clear and intense shade of blue.

I have long been fond of lighthouses, seeking them out whenever I'm by the sea, but this will be the first time I've had a chance to look inside one on a guided tour. As buildings, they possess an irresistible romance. A lighthouse is a landmark of imagination – I feel now as if I could be stepping directly into the pages of a book: the *Lighthouse Keeper* stories that my children so loved when they were small; or Woolf's *To the Lighthouse* (although that iconic lighthouse, with its 'silvery, misty-looking tower' is only ever seen from the outside). The lighthouse here before me also recalls the image I saw carved on the tombstone of Percy Palmer, keeper of the River Severn lights: its classic form traditionally emblematic of light and safety. A coastal lighthouse exists in liminality – it is perched at the borderline of land, sea and sky, a steady point in an ever-flowing weatherscape. There is nowhere fog represents danger more strongly than at sea – to an imperilled ship in the fog a lighthouse can be both guide and protector. And while many lighthouse foghorns have now been decommissioned, this particular lighthouse remains a beacon of light and of sound.

Start Point Lighthouse was first illuminated in 1836, and for a number of years before the two houses (the North and South Dwellings) were built, the lighthouse keeper lived here in the tower accompanied by his family and an assistant keeper. The lighthouse's cramped, curved rooms with their narrow windows are strung together by the winding thread of a spiral staircase that forms the tower's spine. This isolated location, our tour guide tells us, meant it was seen by some keepers as being a 'punishment posting'. As we clatter up the stairs, I peer out through a window and envisage the peninsula draped in cold, damp sea fog – the world beyond unseen, and the sound of the original fog bell dolefully chiming. On the first floor, we come to the kitchen and – in an oddly touching vignette – the table is set for tea: an embroidered tablecloth, a teapot, and pasties on plates. In lighthouse life, the everyday coexisted fully with the elemental.

Climbing further, and stepping into the Flag Room above the kitchen, I find myself staring into an enormous, glittering glass eye. This unexpectedly gorgeous, prismatic structure is the catadioptric lens that lit the lighthouse for sixty years until it was replaced by a (comparatively unpoetic) LED lantern in 2019. Catadioptric lenses are based on an optical system developed by Augustin Fresnel, which uses the refractive and reflective properties of glass 'bullseye' lenses and prisms to collect and focus light into a concentrated horizontal beam – these giant jewels are known as Fresnel Lenses. Unlike traditional lenses, they can capture and focus around 85 per cent of a lamp's available light, allowing a beam to shine much further across the sea, and to potentially be seen through more layers of fog. The lens's multitudinous crystal glass surfaces throw out light patterns onto the walls and ceiling. It winks and beckons me closer to see the tiny rainbows hidden within. Mesmerisingly intricate, it is a rare instance of humans successfully harnessing the elusive magic of light – a secret, a symbol, a miracle of sorts.

As we ascend the steep, slippery ladder, I am so focused on

my feet that I don't realise I have reached the Lantern Room until I take a last step upwards and gasp, finding myself in a diamond-cut prism of never-ending light, floating above fathomless sea below. A tiny yacht bobs by, skirting the headland, sails as white as the lighthouse parapet that stands firm beyond the tessellated windowpanes. Affixed to the parapet is a neat, wired cylinder – this, the tour guide tells us, is the electric fog signal emitter. It's difficult to imagine something so small producing a sufficiently loud noise to reach the yacht below, let alone a distant ship, but in fact it is so powerful that guests in the North and South Dwellings (now holiday lets) must be issued with ear defenders to protect against its might. Issuing a blast every thirty seconds, its signal range is a nautical mile. Yet again, I scan the horizon in search of fog but I see only that cerulean fade which Rebecca Solnit calls the 'blue of distance'.

Also mounted onto the parapet is a fog detector, a piece of equipment that constantly monitors the atmospheric density between its two sensors. When it senses a drop in visibility, this unit sends a message that causes the electric fog signal to sound. To test its efficacy – to simulate fog – a grey circular paddle can be placed between the sensors. Fog here is reduced to pure visibility – representing nothing more or less than levels of clarity between two points. But while a fake representation of fog can emulate atmospheric density, fog's atmospheric moods are more difficult to recreate.

In the past, our guide tells us, the lighthouse keepers sat down at a desk every three hours to complete a weather log. If they judged visibility to be below three miles (using as marker points a white house by day and the lights of an inn by night), they would manually activate the fog signal. This was a labour-intensive task, and in prolonged fog all keepers were needed to stand by. The lighthouse's fog signal had many iterations over the decades: the original fog bell was operated by a heavy weight which, when dropped, caused the clapper to strike the bell for around four and a half hours. In 1876, the bell was upgraded to a compressed-air siren, its coal-fuelled engines contained in a circular engine room. Mounted on the signal house roof were twin bell-mouthed trumpets, which blasted sound. In the same way that each lighthouse light has its own 'character' – flashing in a specific sequence to aid orientation and navigation – each lighthouse's foghorn had a particular voice, a pattern of sound and silence. The curved trumpets were replaced in 1928 by a deep-toned diaphone, its engines stored in the same circular room, until 1983 when cracks appeared in the foundations. The engines were stripped down and removed and a new electric fog signal was installed. In 1989, violent storms left the fog signal engine room sliding down the cliffside, a year later slipping into the sea. The lighthouse stood stalwart, but for the fog signal engine room, the elements had won.

Up in the lighthouse service room, one floor below the lantern, a map shows known shipwrecks in the waters around Start Point, and they are many. The listed names sound a strange and terrible recitation – a found poem:

Reliance
Gossamer
Lizzie Ellen
Lyra, Freedom, Dryad
Spirit of the Ocean

There are, I later learn at the Shipwreck Treasure Museum in Charleston, a total of around 1,600 shipwrecks sunk off the Devon coastline, while Cornwall's waters are a ships' graveyard of over 3,000 wrecks. Although numerous dangers could, and do, precipitate shipwreck – storm or war, for example – a recurring cause (as with the River Severn collision) was undoubtedly fog, given its immediate and unpredictable capacity to render vessels sightless. Fog could obscure land, sun, sea and – at night – the stars. Ships were in danger of being subsumed by silent fog, becoming disorientated and hitting rocks, colliding with other vessels or running aground. This was what fog signals (bells, trumpets, electric emitters) were intended to prevent. To a ship engulfed in fog, the sound of a foghorn indicated that the coast was near and the crew not without aid, but the sound (difficult to reliably pinpoint) could not be used alone as a means of navigation – the voice of a foghorn offered not a guide, but a warning.

Long before the invention of the foghorn, a naturally sounding fog signal existed on a reef known as Wolf's Crag, west of Land's End in Cornwall. A rock stood in this dangerous spot and the waves, washing through a hollowed-out cavern within it, made a wolf-like howling sound that kept ships away. It has been suggested that nearby wreckers (for whom shipwrecks would have been a source of income) may at some point have stopped up the cavern with stones to prevent its sound from alerting sailors to danger. Not long after Start Point Lighthouse was built, a granite lighthouse tower was constructed on Wolf Rock; with its protective light and a fog bell to replace the wind's howl, it offered one more isolated beacon along the dangerous coast.

Beneath those same waters between Land's End and the Isles of Scilly is said to lie a mythical kingdom from Arthurian times called the Lost Land of Lyonnesse, its towns, churches and cathedral having all been swallowed up by the ocean in a single night in a similar watery fate to the kingdom of Cantre'r Gwaelod. Some stories say that on calm days the sound of Lyonnesse's church bells can be heard ringing out beneath the waves, but local legend also tells of another unearthly sound – a fae fog warning known as the Whooper of Sennen Cove. If sea fog suddenly fell, a strange whooping sound was said to be heard from the sea near the village of Sennen. In some tellings the whooping originated from a guiding spirit, a protector from the danger of the fog; in others the sound emanated directly from the fog itself. One day, the story goes, two fishermen ignored this whooping and instead sailed blithely on into the fog: they were never seen again.

After my lighthouse tour, I spend a sea-lulled night in a clifftop chalet overlooking Porthtowan Bay, and the next morning I make my way down to Sennen. The sky is clear, although fog is forecast for later in the day, further up the coast. But passing Penzance, I make a sudden turn down to the seafront – from the road it is apparent that fog has settled over the sea. I stop beside Jubilee Pool, a distinctive white Art Deco sea-water lido. A couple of summers ago, I swam here in the sea off the headland, just behind the lido at Battery Rocks. It was a soft, misty dream of an August morning swim, with sparkles on the water and haze on the horizon. In the distance, the island castle of St Michael's Mount rose up like a vision from the mist, and I watched it as I floated in calm, clear water. Today, the air is heavy – fog hangs over the sea like a smoke-grey blanket. I watch a flock of gulls fly in and land in formation on the water, but the towering castle that I know to lie beyond has vanished as if it was never there. On the next headland, the little lighthouse that sits on the far edge of Newlyn Harbour is barely visible. I close my eyes momentarily and hear growling wind, waves hitting the seawall, and rain dropping into the sea. The dampness is all-encompassing; this fog tastes salty and it is indistinguishable from the rain or the splashing sea; they merge together, flowing and melding.

Pulling out of Penzance, I drive on, the road surface slick and shiny with moisture. In the Cornish countryside, fields have disappeared into fog. Beside the edges of the hedgerows blooms more Allium triquetrum, which (like the china clay trails on Dartmoor) shines white and shows the way. The sea, I know, is out beyond the fields, but the fog is already too dense to see through, and the closer I get to the end of the land, the thicker it becomes. On Sennen Beach, the lifeguards are on duty, their yellow rescue board propped on the sand, a few scattered surfers in the water. The sea on this side of the coast is calm, only raindrops texture its surface. I listen hard, trying to catch a whooping on the wind, but hear only the water gently lapping, the cries of the gulls, and – familiar as a lullaby to a girl who grew up beside Dartmoor – raindrops plopping on my raincoat hood. Along the coast between Sennen Cove and Land's End lies a comparatively recent shipwreck – the *RMS Mülheim* ran aground in Gamper Bay on a foggy morning in March 2003, although it seems to have been an unfortunate accident rather than the foggy conditions which caused the incident. The wreck is visible from the cliffs, and I have seen photographs of the deteriorated vessel in its resting place. For reasons I don't fully understand, shipwrecks make me shudder – perhaps I have been reading too much about souls lost at sea, or perhaps I want to retain my sense of fog as immersive, not destructive – but I know I can't bear to see the immense, twisted metal carcass lying at the foot of the cliff. With rain falling in sheets now, I choose not to take the clifftop path, but head in the opposite direction in search of seascapes.

A woolly mantle of fog sits on the small town of St Just. Like Sennen, this is a place I have visited many times in the happy Technicolour of a summer day. Today, fog has drained the town; the war memorial stands sentinel over empty, muted streets. Down a pretty back lane is the Jackson Foundation Gallery, a carbon-negative art space created by artist Kurt Jackson to celebrate the relationship between art and the natural world. It has high ceilings and tall windows, which last summer looked out onto trees and the hills beyond. Today, they frame a total absence of line or colour, and fog drifts in through the high open door of the gallery. Jackson's art is incredible and, fully surrounded by his paintings, I feel the prickle of tears, having long loved his work. These canvases capture the drama and ever-changing beauty of sea and sky. They are full of light and life: crepuscular glow, sparkles and reflections, coastal colour washes, swirls and smudges of cloud. Often in the corner of his paintings one can see brief pencilled notes recording sense impressions – jotted observations of the moments that make these multi-sensory seascapes, incorporating movement and sound. I pause in the centre of the room – it feels enchanted, with the paintings within and the fog without, and I am momentarily wrapped in wonder. Afterwards, I make my way down the lanes, heading for one last lighthouse. The fog is even heavier now – my eyes can't quite focus and I strain to see. More white alliums glow, welcoming and plentiful along the roadside, and as I pull into the car park, the pale form of the Pendeen Lighthouse tower suddenly looms up on the edge of the clifftop, bearing a weighty shawl of fog.

Standing alongside the cliff, my raincoat is flapping. The wind whips my hair and whistles in my ears. Below me, the water is turquoise – so clear I can make out rocks beneath its surface. Up on the cliff, the rocks are ashen, mottled with neon lichen and surrounded by pompom-pink sea thrift. I'm alone up here but at the top of the lighthouse tower, I realise, the lens is lit. Mounted on a small building in front are the large, curved twin horns of the Pendeen Foghorn, pointing out to sea. Black against the sky, it resembles a crouching, horned mythical beast. Visibility today is certainly below three miles – and in the not-so-distant past, these horns would have been blowing, waves of sound surrounding me, passing out across waves of water.

Foghorns are unique in their melding of weather and sound – fog being probably the only weather condition to have an artificial auditory accompaniment. But all along the coast, foghorns have now fallen silent, growing fewer and fewer as boats increasingly rely on satellite navigation systems, with the crews of larger ships now sealed in to closed bridges, away from the possible guidance of sound. This Pendeen Foghorn was decommissioned in 2014, just one year after fifty ships had gathered on the North Sea to 'mark the disappearance of the foghorn from the sound of the UK's coastal landscape' by performing a unique and ambitious musical score that incorporated 'sense landscape, memory and space'. *Foghorn Requiem* was performed live to audiences on the cliffs by a collective of three brass bands, ships at sea and the Souter Lighthouse Foghorn. Just as fog interacts with landscape, so too did the foghorn – for long years its doleful wail was an integral part of the soundscape of the sea.

Now, down on the foggy sea, a solitary yacht is passing with its spinnaker up, billowing white. Although they are likely to be using GPS to navigate, do the crew look up at the lighthouse on the cliff above, its light spinning on through the grey? The noise of a foghorn has often been described as melancholy, but it seems to me that there's something even more melancholy about a foghorn that doesn't sound at all, standing silent on a clifftop in heavy fog. I try to recall the voice of this elegant foghorn from recordings I've heard, and imagine its sound echoing across the sea, down to the yacht. Leaning forward into the wind, my arms are stretched, I am so small against the vastness. Gulls wheel over my head, riding the wind, and I too feel something like freedom in abandoning myself to the weather. A cormorant slips into my eyeline, landing sleekly on the surface. Landscape and seascape merge here with wind and fog into a wild interconnected weatherscape. Water is everywhere – puddles on the cliff, droplets in the air, waves lashing below. As my fog-self, I relish this combination of fog, wind and salt – coating my skin, twisting my hair and creeping into my ears. Through the coldness I hear the crying of gulls, wind buffeting and waves pummelling rock, but the foghorn makes no sound. For a moment the yacht is visible, flitting between the lighthouse and the foghorn, but then it's gone – out of my sight into the fog – and I'm alone on the clifftop with the pirouetting light.

Down in front of the lighthouse, I unexpectedly notice a dog and, beside it, a small boy in a white football strip, kicking a ball against a wall. I blink, wondering if he could be a figment of my imagination. He is the same size as my own football-loving lad, at school a few counties away. His shirt glimmers, bright against the murky air, and when I hear the familiar thud of a ball repeatedly slamming against a wall, I know that this is no fog figment – the lighthouse boy is real.

When I return home, sitting in my study at the top of the house, my boy kicking his ball in the garden below, I will listen to a recording of *Foghorn Requiem*. Swelling, elegiac music will fill the small room, punctuated by the powerful, eldritch note of the foghorn. Miles away from the ocean, I will close my eyes and let it wash over me, an intermittent, body-shaking bellow. I will think of the silent foghorn on the clifftop, the salt on my skin, the cloak of fog. It is noise I felt only by its absence. Foghorns provide a soundtrack to fog, but to me they are not a voice for it. A foghorn creates a crevice, breaking open fog's silence.

Foghorns are gradually passing into obsolescence but fog remains – for now, although perhaps not forever. We live in a warming world with coastal fog thought to be in decline, at least in some areas. If sea fog should disappear one day, would anyone compose a requiem? I wonder if its loss would even be mourned – are there other fog lovers who see its beauty? Do they too see their fog-selves? Some might consider themselves glad to see it go. Before the foghorn, and later GPS, a foggy day at sea was deeply dangerous – the bottom of the ocean beckoned. The Shipwreck Treasure Museum is filled with poignant items retrieved from sunken ships: brass candlesticks, leather shoes, jet buttons, brass keys, coins, thimbles, buckles, guns and shot. To me, the most haunting sight was a set of intact china plates and bowls, found barnacle-encrusted on the seabed. The salt-softened colours and pocked, lunar surface of this once elegant crockery sent a shiver through me at the quotidian horror of the sea's sunk plunder.

Along the Devon and Cornwall coast, shipwrecks were not always considered to be accidental; myths of wreckers eddy and whirl. The term 'wrecking' is used in Cornwall today, but its meaning is much closer to that of 'beachcombing' – referring to a search for any kind of found item among the shoreline flotsam. By this definition I myself may be a wrecker, finding it impossible to walk along a shore without scanning the tideline for treasure – the shelves beside my fireplace groan with my pickings: cowrie shells, sea glass, smooth pebbles, a mermaid's purse, a sea urchin skeleton, a driftwood heart. The more dastardly elements of wrecking's lurid past – stories of murderous figures waiting on the shore with false lights, ready to deliberately lure ships to their doom – seem to have little basis in fact. They may in part have been popularised by Daphne du Maurier's bleak narrative of pitiless wreckers, a treacherous lantern, and a ship dashed on the rocks in thick fog: *Jamaica Inn*. Turning this book's pages in the clifftop chalet, the murmur of the sea in my ears, I am struck by both how horribly unsettling and how insistently foggy the novel is. In her travelogue memoir *Vanishing Cornwall*, du Maurier describes an incident that inspired her novel. On a November afternoon, she set off with her friend on horseback from Jamaica Inn to ride across the moor and pay a call, but the weather suddenly turned. They found themselves lost, sheltering in an abandoned cottage in decreasing visibility that turned to 'dank fog'. Eventually, the pair decided to remount and loose their horses' reins, in the hope the creatures might lead them through the fog back to the Inn. Happily, they did: du Maurier was returned safely to Jamaica Inn where a fire was waiting, with eggs and bacon for supper and a pot of 'scalding tea'.

When fog appears in the novel *Jamaica Inn*, evil is near. Fog rises up around Mary Yellan as she walks alone on the moor, and it is there, in the confounding mist, that she first meets the ghostly cryptic figure of Francis Davey, vicar of Altarnun. This fog that Mary encounters on Bodmin Moor is not sea fog but a sudden, swaddling moorland fog – like the fog on Dartmoor it obscures paths, tors and bogs alike, making orientation difficult. Mary's rescuer becomes, by the end of the book, her captor, and she once again finds herself in a moorland fog that clings around her 'like a spider's web'. Caught by its tendrils, she can escape neither the fog nor the man. It is not until the fog lifts, and visibility returns, that she is rescued. Sea fog in the novel is perhaps even more evil-infused than the moorland fog. It is with the coast covered by impenetrable fog that Mary, hiding behind a rock, sees wreckers cast their false light from the cliff. The mist lifts, but the night is black, and the lantern, a dark star, lures an unwitting ship onto the rocks, where it splinters and sinks, disgorging its contents to the screeching men on the shore who gleefully pull bodies, goods and wreckage from the waves, with Mary powerless to stop them. Du Maurier's fog is desolate and dangerous – a gothic nightmare – a primal force of evil that seems to emanate from the land itself.

On the way back from Cornwall, I stop at the real Jamaica Inn, its old stones perched atop Bodmin Moor, in between Cornwall's north and south coasts and surrounded by little more than gorse and sheep. This building, now a pub with a small museum, is said to be haunted, and I can certainly imagine feeling unsettled here on a bleak and foggy night. Most interesting to me are the museum's du Maurier exhibits – a small room contains the author's writing desk, her typewriter and a number of other belongings, including a portrait of her as a young woman of sixteen. Standing slightly slumped, her face framed by a thick blonde fringe, she stares thoughtfully into the distance. Du Maurier, who lived in Cornwall for many years, was certainly familiar with sea fog. In *Vanishing Cornwall*, she describes visiting Madron Well (once thought to have been a magic healing spring) with her son. Afterwards, on their way to Penzance, they are caught in a sea mist, the coming of which she describes as 'sad, symbolic of a vanishing age' – this obscuring fog in some way representative of the dense fabric of time. She retells a Cornish legend about an old mansion called Penrose, in which mist and fog rolling in from the sea signify the frightening coming of a once-shipwrecked ghost. In du Maurier's Cornwall, fog was not benign. A few weeks later, I mention to Annie that I have read *Jamaica Inn* for the first time, and she recalls that reading the novel in her teens was the reason she always makes sure to leave the moor before dark – unable to shake the horrors that Mary encountered in the fog.

The moor, and the fog, seem far away as we sit in warm sunshine on an all but empty beach. I am visiting Annie with my family for a long weekend in North Devon. Her local beach, Saunton Sands, is somewhere we have been together endless times since we first met in our teens. It's special for numerous reasons, but particularly for its dreamlike reflections. When the tide goes out on a clear day like this, Saunton's expanse of sand becomes a glassy pond, mirroring the sky. Clouds, surfers, dog walkers and sandcastle diggers are reflected in its shining surface. Today is no different; the sun flares and the beach dazzles. Dan and our sons play perpetual cricket, as Annie and I sit chatting, idly watching the light on the sand and the distant crash of the waves. Suddenly she sits up straight. 'Look,' she says. 'Sea fog.' I narrow my eyes. Could it just be heat haze, wavering above the slick of wet sand? No, she's right – the small figures in the distance have begun to float – around their ankles swirls a low-level, fast-moving cloud of fog, coming in fast. We get to our feet and walk towards it.

Fog is rolling off the sea like smoke, wispy and white. Slowly at first – coiling tendrils, dancing over the waves – and then faster, more insistently. I taste salt in the air, thick on my lips. The rising fog clings to me, leaving its residue on my skin. It's becoming harder to differentiate between sky, sea and fog. At the end of the beach, the green cliffs remain visible but fog is drifting past them in waves, and I look back at my boys, playing in front of a row of coloured beach huts. The fog is spreading, multiplying, changing: it's no longer discernible as individual twists; it has become an all-encompassing cloud. I am standing halfway down the beach, and when I turn back to the sea, it has disappeared from my sight. I can see only a few metres ahead of me now – beyond that, in every direction, there is a white covering of salty fog. I hear a muted roar that could be the sea, or perhaps it's the wind – I can't be sure. Everyone around me has gone; I am adrift in the fog. One by one the surfers walk back up the beach, carrying their boards, passing in and out of my vision like mirages in the mist.

I did not chase this fog, but it found me. On the sunniest of days, fog has appeared from nowhere, rising suddenly out of the sea, wrapping the beach tightly, blocking the sunshine and muffling the light. It is an eerie transformation – in a matter of minutes the place has gone from cheerful beach scene to unearthly whiteout. 'I haven't seen this for years.' It's Annie, materialising from the mist. 'The last time there was sea fog, you were here,' she tells me. I remember it then – the lifting clouds, the floating figures, the white hotel on the clifftop glowing through. Somewhere inside me, my fog-self is rising. 'We've been chosen,' she whispers. 'The fog is calling us.' This sudden submergence feels quite different to my usual deliberate infiltrations into fog. When I chase the fog I am in control – I have chosen where to go, and when, determining what to wear and what to take (my camera, for instance, which I did not bring with me to the beach). Ordinarily, I make a choice to step into the fog's embrace. Today, the fog has taken me, along with everyone else, completely by surprise. I am relieved that it arrived when my children were safely on the sand – the sea, I know, is not a place to be in the fog. I am unsettled, but also slightly thrilled. Has the fog come here for me?

Fog, particularly when it is unexpected, untethers us: it can leave us feeling anchorless – lost at sea. But perhaps I chase fog because this weightless drift is what I hope for. In the fog I'm not a mother, a wife or a writer. I'm neither old nor young, nor even fully corporeal. I'm just there, floating, surrounded by an elemental force. Fog is a space and a sensation – somewhere to be, something to touch but never to hold. Its unpredictable momentariness means that every foggy instant is precious – an offering of sorts. I can't step out of the fog and come back to it later: it won't be there. There is only now, the present. Fog is meditation: a clearing of the mind, a condensing of the experience of the moment. In the fog is nothing but the rhythm of the breath and the counsel of the senses. To be in the fog is to surrender. This is where I am most myself – my true self, my fog-self, is who I find there. But now, on the beach, the light is returning, the sea fog is lifting, the waves are flickering into focus. My youngest son runs up to me with his bodyboard, and my fog-self slips away once more.

I found sea fog (more, even, than I anticipated), but I did not hear a foghorn. Only the wash of waves was audible to me through the stillness. Although it softens vision, fog in itself does not muffle sound – its water molecules are not close enough to affect transmission. In fact, my own experience has been that (perhaps because my sight is restricted) sounds appear clarified when fog falls. The sound I most readily associate with fog is not a foghorn, but birdsong. Walking in the woods one foggy morning, I see a dancing flock of chaffinches dart from branch to branch, ducking and diving, gathering in the trees. As I pass along the path, more twirl up from the ground ahead of me, chattering. The only other sound I can hear is my own gentle footfall, and more birds startle as I walk quietly by: a small flock of pigeons flies up from the leaf-covered ground; two wrens flutter in the hedgerow; a sparrow flits from tree to tree and, on the other side of the field, in a solitary tree, jackdaws caw. There is something in this croaky sound that magnifies fog's strangeness. Often it is the voices of the jackdaws, gathered in the beech tree opposite my study window, that alert me to fog's arrival in the town. From beech bower to rooftop perches they call to one another, and even when the fog grows so thick that the tree disappears from my sight, I hear them, a disembodied echo. In the fog, the street is theirs alone.

Weeks later, it is early in the morning and, after waking to fog and the jackdaws' alarm call, I have returned to St Arilda's hilltop churchyard above the River Severn. The fog is dense, and in the quietude the graveyard is a little unsettling. Below me in the valley I notice a doe, poised and silent on this fog-drenched day. She steps delicately through dewy grass, crossing the field. Hearing me move, she pauses and turns her head to look up. We study each other for the briefest of seconds and then she walks through the hedge, and away. Crows call to each other from the tops of dripping trees. I know that below me lie the river, the power station and the two Severn bridges, but I can barely see beyond the edge of the field. This fog is all-consuming, and yet I can be sure of the direction of the river because, echoing through milkiness, I unexpectedly begin to make out the sound of a foghorn issuing from the mouth of the river. It produces a long slow blast, with a pause before a second long slow blast. Out on the estuary it is high tide – fog is a threat, the foghorn a protector. Its voice is mournful and desolate – it sounds to me like the call of the immense creature I imagined on the clifftop – my artist friend described it as the lowing of a cow in pain. Despite a faint electronic undertone, the sound is a cry, a sadness, a keening. It reverberates across the fog-smothered valley, twisting around me and tethering me, fascinated, to the spot. In its pauses, the countryside inhales – water drips, crows caw. I wait – and then it's back again, the call of the foghorn, live in my ears at last. It is insistent, gloomily bewitching and, like the fog itself, deeply uncanny.

6

SCENT OF THE SEA – EAST COAST OF SCOTLAND

(haar – advection fog – sense of smell)

'What kind of weather do you want to summon?' asks the woman behind the counter in the magical supplies shop, with a smile. 'Oh,' I reply, a little tentatively, plucking at the sleeve of my sundress where it has stuck to my arm, 'well, I was hoping for fog.' It is Midsummer, St John's Day – Litha in the Pagan Wheel of the Year. Magic feels close by; a drifting incense-scent seems to be following me, with the recurring appearance of signs, literal and metaphorical, but fog (although I am in Edinburgh to chase it) has never felt further away. The sky is sharp blue and the dark stone of the city radiates a heat that has been building for days. Across the globe, temperatures have been hitting record highs, as human-caused warming exacerbates the effects of El Niño. In the oceans, including those around the UK, an alarming burst of warmth is resulting in unprecedented high sea surface temperatures. Weather is on everyone's lips: 'Hot, isn't it?' people mutter, searching for shade in parks and gardens and ducking into air-conditioned shops for a blast of chill. The sustained, powerful sunshine – far beyond pleasant Midsummer warmth – is unnatural and unsettling. It is weather as threat.

I have come to the east coast of Scotland in search of the opposite of sunshine – I hope to experience a specific fog, called a haar. During the spring and summer months, this coastal fog is formed when warm, moist air moves over the cool surface of the North Sea and condenses. If the wind is blowing from the east, a sea fret – known locally as haar – will cover the land along the coast. Haar is a milk-white fog, sometimes arriving quickly and unexpectedly, with sunbathers sitting up to find themselves in the midst of mist. Beaches, coastal towns and the entire city of Edinburgh can be subsumed for hours or occasionally for days. The speed at which the haar (a type of advection fog) dissipates again will depend on wind strength and direction, as well as the temperature of the land and how quickly it warms the air – if the land is cool and there is no wind, haar can linger, listless and smoke-like.

The haar is a part of both the physical and cultural character of this coast. In a 2013 article for the *International Journal of Intangible Heritage*, Benjamin Morris suggested that local residents' attachment to the haar 'creates strong connections of local identity, past experience, sense of place, and historicity'. He made the case for considering haar a form of natural heritage, emphasising the need for investigating and documenting it, as well as attempting 'climate mitigation efforts' in order to safeguard it. What if this approach could be applied, not just to the haar, but to each of the different types of fog I seek? I am attempting to document fog, but each time it fades from my sight, I always wonder if this will be the last time I see it.

In the welcome evening cool as I push open the door to the flat in Portobello (Edinburgh's seaside quarter), a jingle sounds from chimes hanging on the back. The clinging smell of incense hits me, a nostalgic aroma from my patchouli-scented teens. On the sideboard sits a brass gong bowl, and another containing angel cards. I draw one out: creativity, it reads. The following morning, opening the bedroom window, I smell sea salt on the breeze. I pull another angel card before leaving to catch the bus into the city. This one is blank: an absence, a white emptiness – fog? From the top deck of the bus I notice a poster on a wall near Waverley Station: a place that exists only in moonlight, it reads. But there are no cool beams of moonlight here, only relentless sun through the windows. Inside the bus, steam drips and, as I alight, hot dry air hits me with a whiff of fried food and the dust of the streets.

Edinburgh has a history of strong smells: hundreds of years ago, the city was christened Auld Reekie (meaning 'old smoky') because smoke from open coal and peat fires hung over it in a thick smog, trapped by the city walls. A damp haar coming in off the sea would have mingled with this smog to form a viscous cloud. Smoke wasn't Edinburgh's only overpowering smell at that time – human waste was emptied into the streets each evening, draining into the Nor' Loch lake. Smoke and street sewage are long gone, but in 2013 Edinburgh was nevertheless named 'smelliest city in the world' by New York-based travel site Thrillist, their complaint being the smells of malt and yeast emanating from the city's many breweries and whisky distilleries.

Dr Kate Mclean has created a visual representation of Edinburgh's unique and not unpleasant smellscape: a scent map entitled 'Smells of Auld Reekie on a Very Breezy Day' in 2011. Smells associated with Edinburgh, primarily those of late spring and early summer, were collected from local residents and included: 'Sea, sand, beach; Brewery malt fumes; Vaults & underground streets; Boys toilets in primary schools; Fish & chip shops; Penguins at the zoo; Cherry blossom; Newly-cut grass; Coffee.' Smells are marked on the map with coloured dots, and co-ordinating contour lines fanning out from each dot show how the smells might spread and mingle across the city in a prevailing southwesterly wind. The shapes created by these smell patterns form an interconnected dance that resembles waves, or perhaps jellyfish – like the huge, copper-coloured 'lion's mane' with its powerful sting spotted in the waters near to where I am staying.

I am familiar with most smells on the map, but brewery malt is a particularly evocative scent for me, as I grew up not far from the Greene King Brewery in Suffolk. Its premises were spread around the town and my younger brother once spent a summer as the brewery postman. Back then, the smell of malt frequently drifted over the streets to our house, but it's not until the end of my first day in Edinburgh that I finally catch a sniff of it here. I stop on the sun-dappled pavement and inhale. Brewery on the breeze – I find it strangely comforting.

One brewery local to Edinburgh produces a beer with a foggy association: the Williams Bros. Brewing Co. in Alloa brews a craft beer called Leann Fraoch (Heather Ale), a version of which has been brewed in Scotland for over 4,000 years. The recipe for fraoch is based on a Gaelic recipe that was brought to the Williams brothers by a woman whose family had handed it down over generations. Following years of testing and development, today's fraoch is brewed using heather flowers with a little myrtle for bitterness, but the original heather ale – as brewed by the Picts – was said to be made from 'heather and some unknown kind of fog'. In my mind I see rows of fog nets strung across Scottish hills, harvesting precious fog droplets to steep with purple heather.

This is not such a far-fetched vision – in Peru and elsewhere, fog-catching does take place today; communities use specially designed fog nets as a means to harvest fog as a source of water in places such as Lima, where rainfall is low but fog is a feature of the local climate. In rural areas, where air is cleaner, this fog can provide drinking water. While the thought of imbibing fog is deeply appealing to me, it seems more likely that the fog used in the Pictish fraoch recipe was a kind of plant – the Scottish National Dictionary includes fog's old meaning of moss or lichen (it mentions the usage in the fraoch recipe, but also moss 'as material in thatching' – which recalls to me Flag Fen). I consider the foggy places I have visited so far, particularly the rainforest fragments; trailing lichen and vibrant moss share more than just a location with fog – woven together by their shared etymological origin, they are parts of the same ecosystem, an interconnected whole. The idea of drinking fog catches at my mind – consuming pure fog-water seems a kind of physical poetry.

There is not a wisp of fog in the Edinburgh streets today, and I stop at the Writers' Museum to read quotations from famous Scottish writers inscribed onto honey-coloured stone paving slabs outside. Nan Shepherd's are the words that speak to me most clearly: 'It's a grand thing to get leave to live.' I walk on, to a second-hand bookshop, in search of my own copy of her nature-writing classic, *The Living Mountain*. Stepping through the low door into silent shade, I inhale the oddly soothing vanilla-sweet smell of slowly decaying paper and walk through a tunnel of book-lined shelves to the desk at the back. They don't have a copy in stock, the bookseller tells me with an apologetic smile. Turning to walk away, I am pulled back by a query that's been hovering at the edge of my consciousness: 'Do you have a section on witchcraft?' I ask. They do, and she takes me there, telling me that if I'm interested in magic, there's also a shop around the corner I could visit. I look at the occult-jumbled shelf in front of me and stop to consider her words. Am I interested in magic? It seems, perhaps, that I am.

It began with a book: *A Spell in the Wild* by Edinburgh-based academic and witch, Dr Alice Tarbuck. In this memoir, a month-by-month exploration of intersectional, accessible witchcraft, I sought an alternative insight into the haar, but unexpectedly found a way to make sense of my fog-self. The book references interactions in which we feel porous: 'as if the world can come not only close against us, but can actually enter right into us' – experiences in which we are changed by the world, and it can be changed by us. I was taken aback; the sensation described is so familiar to me. In the fog – when I exist as my fog-self – I am permeable; the world (the fog) seems to pass into me, becoming part of me. *Yes, this is how it feels*, I think as I read. Alice Tarbuck writes of witchcraft as a way of understanding those inexplicable encounters that are somehow beyond the scope of language. Discovering 'how to court them, how to cause them' is what she defines as magic. Again, I experience the tingle of unexpected connection.

Months ago, I stuck a pencilled note to the wall above my desk – Dr Martin Shaw's words, scrawled down and circled, while watching him speak about art, land and shamanism for 'Tate Modern Lates'. The note reads: 'Courting a weather pattern makes the world magic, electric and deep.' Am I chasing fog, I now wonder – or could I be courting it?

And so it is that I find myself crossing the doorstep of the black-fronted magical shop on Candlemaker Row. It stocks, appropriately, handmade candles, and the small room is a jumble of pleasant, peculiar and indefinable scents. I see smudge sticks, wands, spell jars, crystals of all colours and a small library of magic books – I am here seeking weather spells. Weather magic, the shopkeeper tells me, is unusual. I would need to engage with the elements, channelling in particular the water element. She finds me a book that references elemental magic and tells me about her own magical practice. In creating a spell for fog, she explains, she would think of how to represent fog – by collecting kettle steam in a jar, for example – adding that magic is personal, and I should find my own symbols that make sense to me. *A Spell in the Wild* explained magical symbols as being a kind of metaphor, where one thing shares attributes with something else. If I want to summon fog – to court it – it seems that I must find a simulacrum. Online, I have read that fog's smoke-like attributes can be recreated using incense or a smoky quartz crystal, one type of which is known as a 'Cairngorm' after the Scottish mountain range in which it is found. I rummage through the box of crystals to find a smooth, almost transparent, grey polished pebble that resembles a foggy sky. 'If you do summon fog,' says the shopkeeper, smiling, 'send some our way. It's so hot!'

I nod, thank her, and slip the magic book into my bag, leaving with the smoky quartz clutched tightly in my hand. As I step out onto the pavement, clouds pass over the sun.

Midsummer, the longest stretch of light of the year, was believed to be a particularly potent day for the gathering of herbs and flowers (including heather) but especially yellow St John's Wort (Hypericum), which was thought to be protective if picked at this time. In *The Living Mountain*, Nan Shepherd relates a feeling of enchantment upon finding a gleaming sprig of St John's Wort in a mountain stream, its leaves covered by oil pores that create a layer of sparkling light. As a child, my mum would soothe my cuts with a cream made from Hypericum and (another yellow flower) Calendula. I do not know where to find these particular blooms, but later, in the garden of the modern art museum, I pick a handful of fragrant rose petals and collect a few fallen pine cones – I have read that Wiccan weather spells suggest their usage for fog-summoning. Like the roses, my dress is white; it's one I wear when I take self-portraits in the fog. Wearing white, I feel ever-ready for the arrival of my fog-self, she who shines like quartz pebbles, china clay, alliums or sheep's wool; she who will drift phantasmic between the trees, belonging to the wood, to the fog, to the moment. When I shake her off and return home, the hemline of my dress tells my story, dirtied by splashes from puddles and smeared by muddy leaves; like my skin, it carries an imprint of a walk in the fog. Now, though, in the pine-dry shade of the hot Scottish garden, I find it hard to remember the gently numbing sensation of fog on my skin. I am tense and coiled – my need for fog is becoming heavy, like an ache. Alice

Tarbuck described the way that 'haar holds smell, and wraps it round you' – adding that the sea fog will 'swallow everything you know, to alter it subtly'. This – fog as transformation – is what I am seeking.

When does wishing for fog become summoning fog? Will there come a point where obsession merges into magic? Finding no fog in the city, I return to the water. At the beach in Portobello, the sea smooths the shore with only the tiniest undulations ruffling its surface. Opposite, on the other side of the Forth, I can make out distant mountains. The sky is a wide sheet of gradually fading blue, reflected in the water's lucid teal. It smells of salt and a kind of watermelon freshness. I've been immersed in the fire element all day – the sun, the heat, the incense smoke. I desperately need to return to water's element and am craving chill weightlessness, so I strip down to my swimming costume and wade in. The biting North Sea is a shock – this is several degrees lower than where I swim at home – but as I strike out, the splash on my skin is a kind of bliss. Seabirds glide overhead, and the sun's path is marked out in spangles. I float for a while, my lifted feet gold, my body soothed by cool. Afterwards, wrapped in a towel, I eat a beach picnic for supper. The light is too perfect to miss: pale and slightly milky – like seeing though a sharp-edged crystal.

The next day I wake early. The sky (to my disappointment) is clear, but I am ready to walk part of the North Sea Trail, a long-distance footpath that hugs the North Sea coast. The haar, when it does come, clings tight to the coast: rolling in across beaches and coastal villages in the early morning or evening and dissolving as it reaches further inland. As I walk the coast, I will be following the path of the haar. Today the morning sea remains calm, glinting in patches, and I envy the Sunday morning swimmers. I pass joggers, cyclists and a wooden sauna on a trailer. A group of people are doing yoga on the sand, and three ladies wearing towels, hair sea-damp, pass me on their way up the hill. At the end of the promenade, a terrace of houses opens out onto the seafront, the scent of lavender and roses emanating from their gardens. Poppies and tufts of barley are growing out of the sea wall, with elderflower and valerian down among the rocks. This is where the city meets the wild, where the salt-heavy haar can stretch out and cover the land. At a gap in the sea wall, I find steps down to the water, concrete disappearing into sea. The water calls to me but I keep walking through the edgelands, and pass into East Lothian.

Dog roses grow here along the shoreline at Fisherrow, with thistles and wild fennel. The low dunes swish with marram and lyme grass, and the sand is striped with seaweed and crushed white clam shells. Along the tideline are the morning's offerings – driftwood, pine cones and a single torn bird's wing. Clouds swirl, sombre, and the wind stirs the water, which is many shades of slate. I smell salt-rotted seaweed and hear the clinking of masts from yachts in a little stone harbour. This was a fishing community, a place that depended on the sea – the haar's arrival would once more than likely have meant danger. Now the houses along the seafront have drift-wood on their windowsills and pink roses growing up beside the doors. One gate is decorated with a row of swirled seashells impaled on metal spikes like amulets. When the haar comes in off the sea, it will push insistently against the windows of

these houses like a spreading saltwater ghost. Today, in the
merciless sun, even a slight sea breeze is welcome and I look
once more to the mountains in the distance, where fog feels
at least possible. The gathering heat is increasingly alarming
and now, more desperately than ever, I crave the touch of fog
on my skin. Sea fog (including haar) most commonly occurs
between April and September, but this year it seems I have
chosen the wrong time to come here chasing fog, although in
these times, weather is out of sync everywhere.

Behind me as I walk is the Edinburgh skyline, running
down to the water with the jagged peak of Arthur's Seat in
the background. The city nudges up against the sea, so when
the haar moves along the Firth, it can drift up into Edinburgh,
filling the city with fog. Now the tide is out, and a man, a
boy and a dog are walking across wet sand towards the water.
Turning the corner to Musselburgh Lagoons (an RSPB wetland), I find that a great flock of swans has gathered on the edge
of the sand – I've never seen so many in one place, white wings
against navy sea. What an unexpected sight they would make
in a haar – rising, manifold and spectral out of the fog. Flocks
of blackface gulls fly up from the grass, heading out towards
the water, and a sign warns me to tread carefully as ringed
plover are nesting nearby. Looking down, I count clover and
cornflower, poppies and rosebay willowherb, and I scour the
rocks for seals, but see none. The clouds are so dark that the
sea looks almost black. Then, scrawled across an old, faded
warning sign, I notice some graffiti inscribed in capital letters
using thick, black marker pen. It reads: SHIP ARRIVING
TOO LATE TO SAVE A DROWNING WITCH.

Later, I will discover this to be the name of a Frank Zappa

album, but in the instant it chills me, for this is a place with a bleak history: across the Forth in Torryburn lies the inter- tidal grave of a woman called Lilias Adie, who was accused of witchcraft and, after confessing under torture, died in custody in 1704. Refused final rest in consecrated ground, she was instead buried on the shoreline at low tide, her watery grave weighted down with a stone in a hideous perpetual drowning. Just a little way along the coast from where I stand, the town of North Berwick is known for an earlier series of deadly witch trials with a weather association that took place in 1590–1 at the instigation of King James VI. In *Witchcraft: A History in 13 Trials*, Marion Gibson explains that King James set sail for Denmark to marry Anna, daughter of King Frederick II. His betrothed had been unable to reach Scotland as repeated bad weather made sailing conditions dangerous. A few months later, on the return voyage with his bride, King James found his ship too was plagued by storms. He and his new wife almost drowned and, rather than seeing this as an unfortunate weather event, King James (believing himself to be under threat) took the storms to be the deliberate work of witches. His view was echoed by his wife and the Danish court, and so witch trials were held in both Denmark and Scotland.

More than a hundred witches were tried for the storm raising including, in North Berwick, local women (and healers) Agnes Samson and Geillis Duncan. The trial was un- usual because of the nature of the perceived crime – weather magic – and because the witches were accused of using the occult to plot against the king. It was also notable for the use of sustained and horrific torture – it was under extreme duress that Agnes Sampson and Geillis Duncan eventually confessed to deliberately creating a sea storm with which to threaten the king's ship (and to other incredible things, including a supposed meeting of over a hundred witches inside North Berwick Church). For them, weather-summoning magic proved to carry the most severe and awful of penalties. Both women were found guilty – of witchcraft and of treason – and sentenced to death. Following her imprisonment in Edinburgh Castle, Agnes Samson was publicly executed on Castle Rock – she was strangled and then her body set alight, fire spreading the stench of unjust death: 'People smelled the smoke,' writes Gibson, 'drifting over the city on the east wind.'

Perhaps the most well-known Scottish witches, the Weird Sisters from Shakespeare's *Macbeth* (a play written around fifteen years after Agnes Sampson's death), famously make reference to fog, saying: 'Fair is foul, and foul is fair/ Hover through the fog and filthy air.' Their inversion of good and evil suggests that these witches delight in foulness, filth and fog. They float apart from the world below, observing the action, concealed by foggy fumes. Fog is portrayed as dirty and obfuscating, a shield to evil and a tool of disorder. But the three witches regard fog differently, seeming drawn to it – perhaps they, in their supernatural state, can see in fog something that mortals cannot. Later in the play, one of the witches refers to sailing 'in a sieve', a detail presumed to be derived from the confession of Agnes Samson, who at one point claimed that witches had sailed in sieves to the meeting in North Berwick Church. Appearing to the accompaniment of thunder and lightning, Shakespeare's witches are clearly associated with weather magic, and with chaotic weather more generally – weather that mirrors the unnatural events and unpleasant acts that take place in the course of the play.

Macbeth's strange, wild weather proved to be prescient. Now, in the twenty-first century, dark and unnatural forces do affect the weather, but it's not witchcraft – it's us. The effects of climate change, the UN Secretary General says as I write, are out of control. We are hurtling fast into climate emergency and weather of all kinds is becoming unpredictable, fraught with danger and heavy with new meaning. It isn't just fog that is at threat of vanishing – one day we, like the witch, may be at risk of drowning, or of burning. Witches were condemned to death for controlling the weather, and yet we now find that as a result of our collective actions, weather is being altered in the most alarming way imaginable. Our once clearly defined seasons are beginning to merge, with each season's weather (including fog) changing year on year. In both global and local terms, as weather patterns shift, becoming swiftly unrecognisable, the ways in which we mark time and recognise place will be forced to adjust and reform, engendering in us a deep sense of shared loss. If there is any kind of magic that can now exert change to control the weather, I have to believe that it's reaching the tipping point of collective climate action, led by the tenacity of hope.

I catch the bus into Edinburgh, leaving the coast behind. As I disembark, I can smell rain approaching – an indefinable clean freshness that touches the back of my nose, the answer to an unasked question. I think once more of weather magic – its elemental, physical immediacy. I am mindful that predicting – let alone summoning – the weather is a practice that could once have been dangerous, even deadly, and yet my senses now feel far more attuned to weather than they ever have before. I make my way up through the park towards Arthur's Seat. The unbroken heat feels oppressive and I want to be close to the sky. My path is lined by long grass that hides nesting skylarks, and pink foxgloves sway up from this meadow. I pass a cluster of rowan trees, the last of their blossom fading. Rowan was once believed to be protective against magic, and trees like these, with their orange-red berries in autumn, were planted close to houses to act as a deterrent to witches. People would carry rowan twigs or hang them as defence against enchantment. One of my children is named for the rowan, and so to me this tree represents love.

As I continue to climb, I smell the sweetness of gorse flowers, and the raindrops the sky had promised now begin to fall. Their coolness on my skin is welcome. I stop and look down, across to the far horizon. Past the ships, in a gap between the two edges of land, is the open sea – a faded plane of nothingness from where an approaching haar might originate, but all I see is a floating fleck of cloud. The wind is stronger now, the sky is glowering and rain falls faster. Standing high on an extinct volcano, this incoming weather feels wild and uncontrollable, despite the rain's balm. As I turn to make my way down, a baby magpie – with cerulean wing and tail feathers and a fluffy head – hops onto the path in front of me. It chirps intently for a moment, looking up with shining eyes as if it has something important to tell me, before fluttering away and disappearing into the grass. I ride the bus all the way back in the rain, misted-up windows fogging the world. The city beyond is muffled, traffic lights a diffused glow.

*

There are ways other than magic by which to summon fog – Scottish physicist Charles Wilson (born close to Edinburgh) recreated fog using scientific means through his invention of cloud chambers. As a recent graduate, his emerging interest in clouds took him to the top of a foggy mountain – Ben Nevis, the highest mountain in Scotland. In 1894 he spent the summer there, working as a relief observer at the Ben Nevis Observatory (Britain's highest weather station), which operated from 1883 to 1904. The observatory, situated right on the mountain summit, consisted of a handful of stone-walled rooms and a ten-metre-high wooden tower. Hourly weather observations were recorded by a small team of meteorologists living on site. Like lighthouse keepers, they existed in close quarters. Ben Nevis was an extremely foggy environment – being usually above the base of the clouds, the mountain summit remained enveloped in hill fog for much of the year. In summer, the frequent fog soaked everything exposed to it, causing surfaces to stream with moisture. In winter, low temperatures produced frozen fog crystals – 'long feathery masses of crystalline snow' that coated the tower and could, in particularly dense fog, grow at a rate of two feet a day.

Being situated in a state of almost perpetual fog was not without advantage, however – the Ben Nevis Observatory afforded its residents a rare opportunity to experience the incredible effects of fog and cloud on the light of the sun and moon. A range of optical meteorological wonders were observed and recorded. These foggy phenomena included: coronae (rainbow circles visible around the moon or sun during thin mist); fog-bows (both solar and lunar), and glories (those coloured rings around the head of an observer's shadow). In an account of life at the observatory, glories are described as being commonly seen in winter when standing on the northern side of the mountain and looking into the valley below: 'This deep, gloomy gorge is often full of loose shifting fog, and when the shadow falls upon it, the observer sees his head surrounded by a series of coloured rings.' Usually, the shadow was small: 'the image of the head appears as a mere dark speck in the centre', but sometimes, if conditions were right, the shadow would take on the enlarged, exaggerated form of a Brocken Spectre, haloed by the glories' looped rainbows.

During his time at the observatory, Charles Wilson found himself drawn to the beauty of the glories he saw on the foggy mountain, and when he returned to his laboratory in Cambridge he sought to mimic the effect on a smaller scale by recreating clouds in a controlled environment: a feat he achieved by putting air saturated with water vapour into a sealed container and suddenly expanding the container volume – an invention known as a 'cloud chamber'. Inspired by the otherworldly beauty of glories, Wilson had carried the idea of fog down from the mountain and brought it into being in the laboratory. A plaque on the site of the now-ruined observatory reads: 'The Brocken Spectre seen from here on cloud in the Great Corrie by C. T. R. Wilson in 1894 led him to researches which culminated in the development of the Wilson Cloud Chamber, and for which he was awarded a Nobel Prize in 1927.'

Wilson had been chasing fog (and glories), but his cloud chamber unexpectedly proved to be a crucial development in the study of particle physics. Over the course of almost twenty years of experiments, he discovered that a cloud chamber could be used to detect and reveal radioactive particles – when an ionised particle was present in the chamber, it caused water vapour to condense and form into water droplets around it, revealing a discernible path through the chamber. Charles Wilson made visible the previously undetectable, his work underpinning physicists' current understanding of particle physics. Wilson sought cloudiness but he found clarity – the swirling mountain fog led to a discovery that facilitated a new way of comprehending the structure of the world. It was from my brother Tom, a philosopher of physics, that I first learned of this physicist who generated fog. He told me Wilson's story and showed me a grainy black and white video shot inside a cloud chamber. In the centre of the vapour-filled space I could see the solid silhouette of a small piece of uranium. Shooting from it – like fireworks, or vapour trails – were particles made visible by clinging water droplets. They spread outwards to the chamber's edges, endless cloudy puffs in an unpredictable spiralling dance. I was looking at a box of fog in which the imperceptible had been captured, and it was beautiful. Inside Wilson's Cloud Chamber – inspired by fog and glories, built in a laboratory – poetry and physics meet.

A little north of Ben Nevis, on the Cairngorm mountain range's highest peak, Ben Macdui, folklore tells of an odd, unsettling presence that haunts the fog. It is known as Am Fear Liath Mòr, or the Big Grey Man, and is said to manifest as a dark figure, superhumanly tall and thin. The Grey Man, which has been compared to the Brenin Llywd, has rarely been seen, but climbers have described experiencing a sense of unease while walking in mist, or hearing the crunch of footsteps following them. It seems plausible that a tall, dark figure viewed through fog could have been a Brocken Spectre like those on the neighbouring mountain, but these descriptions of horror are quite different to the wonder experienced by Wilson, and the footsteps remain a mystery. Nan Shepherd, whose book *The Living Mountain* contains her deep knowledge and love of the Cairngorms, also saw a supernatural quality to mist on the mountainside, although her words captured not fear but loveliness: 'Thin mist,' she wrote, 'through which the sun is suffused, gives the mountain a tenuous and ghost-like beauty.' Her familiarity with the mountain landscape and intuitive observations of its weather allowed her to differentiate between, and describe, many kinds of mist: the 'ghastl[y] white' fog that obscured vision; the 'driving mist' that enveloped walkers, and the 'transparent mist' out of which flew a peregrine falcon. Through her words, fog's perpetually shifting shapes revealed the ever-changing mood of the mountains, but she favoured reality over magic, writing of her mistrust of 'glamourie' – a Scottish word meaning bewitchment, dazzlement, a state of unreality – which she saw as creating an artificial barrier between self and world. Does bewitchment contain the sensation of co-mingling world and self, or does it prevent it? There are many various ways for self to commune with world, but my own way is found in the fog.

At the start of September, even in the midst of another Scottish heatwave, I see photographs on Instagram that document the all-encompassing return of the haar. One image, a fog-smothered beach along the same coastline I walked – light-flattened, horizon barely discernible – is captioned 'the sun didn't burn through the haar today'. It is unrecognisable from the shoreline I visited. So often, fog chasing is pure luck – a yearning search for serendipity, a hope to find myself in the right place at the exact foggy moment. I feel frustrated, after my long, hot days by the Forth, to have missed the haar's arrival. But meteorologists too find fog challenging to predict; in the week following the autumn equinox, my weather forecasting app foretells mist on several consecutive mornings but each time it fails to materialise.

On the day of the September 'super harvest' full moon, I note another tentative forecast of mist and decide to attempt a little fog summoning of my own. I place my smoky quartz crystal at the bottom of a clean jam jar, fill it with a cloud of steam from the kettle – as the woman in the magic shop suggested – and seal the lid. Holding the warm jar in my hands, I close my eyes and visualise the woods on the hill filled with fog. 'Bring me fog. Please,' I whisper, a plea to the universe. I place the jar on the windowsill of my loft room study. This is my version of making moon water (water charged with lunar energy from the light of the full moon). I leave the fog jar waiting for moonlight and mist.

The next morning, though, I wake to sunshine and clear skies. Standing in the garden, looking up at a hill without a hint of fog, I take my phone from my pocket to check the current weather forecast. 'Mist', it promises, but there is none. Later, the September scarcity of fog is explained when scientists reveal that worldwide it has been the most anomalously warm month on record. When I wrote that fog was disappearing, I did not expect it to happen so soon. This time last year, I found fog in the woods, the town and in the Severn Valley. This September, although I have heard mutterings of mist, I myself have not experienced a single foggy morning. The change – and the future – feels terrifying. I keep the crystal jar on a shelf in my study, unwilling to give up on either magic or hope. I long for fog, itself a kind of magic; a walk in the fog is a way to become what Sharon Blackie calls 'enmeshed' – fully present, consciously engaged, woven into the web of the world. As September slips into October, fog finally drifts back into town but it stays slightly out of reach, always just a little further down the road from where I stand. As I walk to work in the bookshop, looking up I see that the trees on the far hill are like a mirage – the air is blurred, but although fog promises, it does not materialise.

Finally, gloriously, in early October fog's promise is fulfilled and I wake to a tide of silver-grey. Fog covers the whole town, making its way up the street and through my open loft room window once more. I go to the woods, where spiderwebs cling to the hedges. I can hear the leaves – brittle and dull green – dying on the trees. They crackle as they loosen from the branches and fall. Water drips, a wood pigeon coos and a nuthatch calls loudly. I set up my camera and tripod to try to capture a self-portrait in the fog. I'm wearing my white dress, and a pair of walkers are startled to see me. 'What are you taking photographs of?' one asks incredulously. 'It's misty!' But there are others, regulars in the woods, who are used to seeing me flit between the trees like a lost ghost. I meet the lady who walks a different dog each day. She stops to chat and I tell her that the last passer-by was bemused by my fondness for fog. 'Oh, but it's beautiful!' she says, gesturing to the foggy wood, and walks on – another kindred spirit.

Alongside the path, seed-heads are caught in a matted

tangle of spiderwebs forming a gossamer silk ball, individual strands drifting out and swaying across the path, recalling in their stickiness the clinging Cornish fog of *Jamaica Inn*. On the side of a tree trunk, spiders have made dense hammocks that flex up and down in the wind, and along the thinnest branches, a network of perfect webs glitter with water droplets, each a minute, sparkling world. Spiderwebs, I realise, are another treasure that shine white in the fog, but they are visible only from certain angles, brought into vision by dewdrops – if I turn my head slightly, they disappear.

In the foggy world of Alice Oswald's 'Mist', a crow cries loudly from the top of a tree about the spiderwebs and 'actualities' it finds there. Actuality is the state of existing in reality; the world often feels unreal in the fog but time spent immersed in it can actually intensify our awareness of the true details of reality. Now, the wing-beats of the wood pigeon vibrate the air above me, and a flock of meadow pipits flies across the path, disappearing into the sky. Woven through the hedge, the emerging feathery fronds of autumnal Clematis vitalba glow. I've been out in the fog for two hours now, and it shows no sign of fading. It has erased the horizon and, as I cross the field that adjoins the woods, I feel as if I myself am disappearing. The wind whips the skirt of my dress; the soothing air blows across my face and through my hair. I am calmer and happier than I have been for a long time. I think of the crystal jar on my shelf; I step into my fog-self and I am free. There is nothing now but the feeling of fog – a fading into nothingness.

7

Sensing Other Worlds – Beara Peninsula, Ireland

(féth fíada – mist – sense of intuition)

Van Morrison is singing about a foghorn as I drive the coast road, following the Wild Atlantic Way around Ireland's Beara Peninsula. *Moondance*, my mum tells me from the passenger seat, was an album she first played on vinyl as a sixth former in the Devon seaside town where she grew up, shortly before leaving home to spend three months volunteering in Belfast. This song, so familiar from my own childhood, is called 'Into The Mystic'. Now, the mystic brings to my mind a storyteller sleeping on a foggy Welsh mountain, but somehow, in all the times I heard this song, I had missed the foghorn. Listening again, I realise that this fog-focused song contains layers of meaning and that its foghorn signifies not danger and fear, but love and home: the lyrics describe a sailor returning to his girl, and the foghorn is a sound he longs to hear. The song's original title was 'Into The Misty', which is where we too hope to go.

It is a fair October day and the twisting road takes us past blanket bog and standing stone, skirting the base of Cork's Slieve Miskish Mountains and following a line of coloured vertical prayer flags to a Buddhist meditation centre on the clifftop. I have come to this remote, rugged, breathtaking part of the world in search of mist, with my focus on the sense of intuition: the sixth sense. Meditating is one way to heighten intuition, and my mum, who is a trained yoga and meditation teacher, has found us a guided morning class. She tells me now that meditation is not just about creating internal peace, but is also about projecting peace into the world, and in a week when conflict is raging in Ukraine, Gaza, Sudan and elsewhere, this is something I need to believe.

Clear coastal light fills the meditation room, where seven high panes of glass overlook the sea. In front of the curved window, tree branches are pulled by the wind. Behind them, a twinkling expanse of sea and the silhouette of far mountains. Two rows of straight-backed chairs face the view, with floor cushions in front. Our teacher wears a yellow plaid shirt, a blanket on his knees. Gathered beside him is a small Buddha statue, a burning candle and a picture of the Virgin Mary. The metallic-bright note of a gong cleanses the air, an indication that the first guided meditation has begun. Keeping my eyes lightly open as instructed, I try to rest my mind on a mountain peak framed by branches. We are told to notice our thoughts and then – with great kindness – to send them away, but there are birds outside the window, flying in and out of a wall; the silver-grey sea is in constant rippling motion; clouds froth, and the sun breaks through. Used to collecting my thoughts with words, I am finding it difficult to send them away. I think of Shirley Jackson, who wrote in *Memory & Delusion* that 'a writer is always writing, seeing everything through a thin mist of words'.

The word-mist gathers as I remember my only previous experience of meditation. I was eighteen years old and living in Thailand. I recall sitting on the concrete floor of a forest monastery, the scent of jasmine curling around me, mosquitoes biting my bare ankles. Then, as now, I felt the stretch of an endless-seeming moment. It is not until our third and final guided meditation that my mind clears a little and I experience a few minutes of calm before the gong chimes once more to close the session. 'Have we met before?' the teacher asks Mum on the way out. Perhaps she too has a doppelganger. Not for the first time on this fog-chasing journey, a sense of uncanniness flickers.

We are staying in a square cottage built of grey stone and sandwiched neatly between two outcrops of rock. It sits below the mountains, on the edge of a network of emerald fields in which sheep graze. On the far hillside, a handful of white houses below clumps of fir trees. In the distance, the sea. 'You're lucky you weren't here last week!' exclaims the farmer who owns (and built) the cottage. 'We had rain, and so much fecking fog. Oh, the fecking fog!' I decide not to explain that it was in fact the fog I came here for, only agreeing that the narrow, steep roads of the peninsula must be perilous in thick fog. But even on a sunny day the Beara Peninsula's high incidence of damp weather and fog is evident – this is a landscape saturated with water. Bog stretches between the mountains and the sea, scattered with boulders, heads of bog cotton (now going to seed), orange bog asphodel flowers and pools of tranquil water. Drystone walls are speckled with moss and lichen; roadside grass squelches. The peninsula also has an incredibly high incidence of ancient sites, and the map is liberally dotted with Bronze Age remains: wedge tombs, standing stones, stone circles and more. Beara is rich with history and sacred significance, an ageless landscape where fog has been before and where fog will be again – I have come here to look for mist, but I am also searching for thin places.

Thin places are locations in which the distance between our world and the Celtic dwelling place of gods and ancestors known as the Otherworld is said to diminish, the dividing veil becoming thin and porous, perhaps even passable. In Ireland, thin places are called *áiteanna tanaí*, and writer Kerri ní Dochartaigh describes thin places as sites that 'make us feel something larger than ourselves, as though we are held in a place between worlds, beyond experience'. Thin places are liminal, fluid spaces where the daily can touch the divine and where we may feel the past quiver. They transcend recognised physical experiences – it is through intuition that we perceive a glimpse of something expansive and meaningful, beyond our immediate lived reality: the Otherworld is a 'realm beyond the senses'.

When I first came across the concept of thin places, the sensation was deeply familiar to me although the words were not. I thought of my Dartmoor childhood, and the gnarled hollow trees above the castle in which I often hid to speak to the fairies. I thought of a ruined Thai temple in a silent wood to which – as a young woman grown slight by grief at the death of my best friend – I returned week after week, sitting quietly at the feet of a Buddha statue so intricately weathered it had come to resemble a Giacometti sculpture. I thought too

of the oaken grove of Wistman's Wood, the slopes of Cadair
Idris and the reflective waters of Flag Fen. Places of mystery,
places of peace, places of light.

On our way to Ardgroom stone circle (Dhá Dhrom), we
stop for lunch in Ardgroom village. Over soup and thick brown
bread, I flick through a book of local folk tales that describes
nearby sightings of visitations from the Otherworld – horses,
pigs and a strange glowing light that proved to be not of this
world. Patches of sunlight illuminate the hills, and as we climb
the path to the stone circle the ground is so boggy it bounces.
We cross a trickle of a stream to see the stone circle standing
halfway up the hill surrounded by sheep, a raven sitting silent
on one of the stones. As we approach, sheep scatter and the
bird opens its wings, returning to the air. On an information
board before the stones, I read that stone circles – ritual and
ceremonial sites constructed during the Bronze Age – were
typically orientated according to significant solar and lunar
events and some of the brighter stars; our ancestors were
closely attuned to the changing seasons and the shifting sky.
Circles consisted of an uneven number of free-standing spaced
stones – as with Dartmoor's Nine Maidens. This Ardgroom
circle once had eleven stones but now one is missing and one
has fallen, leaving nine stones on this hillside that overlooks
the wide Kenmare River, with an additional, taller standing
stone a few metres outside the circle, indicating the way.

The stones are flat and tapered, their surface marked by
paint-splatter drips of bird droppings and patches of green
moss – fog's only tangible presence here today; the moss is
simultaneously decorating and devouring the hard stone.
Crustose lichen smoothes the stones in flat, dust-grey patches,

and a lichen I tentatively identify as Evernia prunastri grows on one stone's water-facing side in clusters of seaweed-curling fronds. Resting my face against the stone's rough surface, I look down to the river below and try once more to clear my mind. I feel the solidity of unchanging land beneath my feet and the pressure of stone against my cheek, full of latent power. I hear the calls of sheep, a fierce, buffeting wind that promises rain and, above me, the raven's cry. I taste salt and sky. Closing my eyes for a moment, I experience the same tingle of connection I felt on Cadair Idris – a sense of stepping out of time for an instant, or of catching a brief strain of faint, gorgeous, unfamiliar music on a crackly radio, wavering in the space between stations. When I open my eyes, I see that a rainbow has appeared in a patch of sunlight on the hills beyond the river. It is not an arc but a blurred mass of colour that swiftly fades, vanishing into the hillside. After we walk away, the sheep return to their grazing place in the circle and the stones belong once again to the raven.

In Celtic mythology there is a magic mist called féth fíada. It grants invisibility to those it covers, and the ability to summon it belongs to druids and to the Tuatha Dé Danann, an elusive race of Irish immortal divinities. Myth tells that the Tuatha Dé Danann were supernatural beings who lived under the surface of the landscape, in hills and mounds called sídhe. These fairy mounds, unassuming from the outside, led to an interior mirror world containing palatial dwellings furnished with sparkling crystal chairs, and idyllic lands of unearthly beauty, sometimes including the realm of the Otherworld. By assuming féth fíada's veil of invisibility, the Tuatha Dé Danann could emerge from these concealed caverns and walk among mortals undetected. Their mist was also associated with spells of transformation – it could be used to assume animal form – meaning that the peninsula's Otherworldly visitations of pigs and horses may have been attributed to it. Féth fíada is connected in particular with Manannán mac Lir, a sea-deity who wore a sea-shimmered, colour-shifting cloak, like light on the surface of the ocean, and who used his magical mist to conceal himself from his enemies. It is Manannán mac Lir who was said to have first given the power of féth fíada to the Tuatha Dé Danann, and in the Irish Sea – on the Isle of Man – a thick concealing fog is referred to locally as 'Manannan's cloak'.

In some stories, Manannán mac Lir was husband to the Cailleach, an elder deity of Irish and Scottish mythology whose name means 'old woman', 'hag' or 'veiled one'. Traditions of the Cailleach vary from place to place; in many tellings she is not only a wise ancestor – the archetypal old woman – but also a creator-goddess who scatters stones from her apron that turn to mountains as she walks. In these versions of her story, wilderness is her domain; she moulds and shapes the land, forming and protecting it. The Cailleach was thought to have had the power to regenerate, passing from old age back to youth again. She is often considered to be a seasonal spirit associated with cold wet weather. In these stories she personifies winter – sometimes referred to as Queen of Winter – presiding over the dark months of the year and summoning storms and snow. With a name that means 'veiled one', and having a predilection for wild weather, I imagine that the Cailleach must be a friend to fog. As weaver of weather, I presume she even has the power to summon fog. Surely she – Queen of

Winter, wife of a mist-making sea-god – could have something to teach my incipient fog-self? It may be for this reason that I feel particularly drawn to her. There are a number of physical locations in Ireland and Scotland associated with the Cailleach, one of which is not far from our cottage on the Beara Peninsula – a large rock called the Hag of Beara, which stands on the cliff overlooking Coulagh Bay.

My mum's raincoat is the same shade of blue as the sky, as she stands on the Kilcatherine Peninsula in front of the Hag of Beara, looking out to sea. Below her is a tiny rocky island, and two bobbing fishing boats are moored on the bay where glittering ripples drift inland. The coast road curves along the shoreline and sheep wander through marshy ground that runs down to the sea. At the edge of the land stands the bulbous boulder, which legend tells us is the Hag – the Cailleach – petrified into stone. Stories about her fate vary, but the one I choose to believe says that she is waiting here for her husband – her misty love Manannán mac Lir – to return from the sea. Mum, a volunteer for the local wildlife trust who works on habitat maps, has bent down to examine the plants at her feet. Between the layers of clifftop rock, lichen and moss grow here, a miniature forest of varying shades and textures: pale coral skeletal, vivid green succulent, and feathery emerald organisms sandwiched in between the layers. She turns then towards the Cailleach and I see her reach out her hand. Over the buffeting wind I hear the high cries of meadow pipits, and then my mum's voice calling me. 'Laura, look. People have left her gifts.'

From behind, the rock appears solid and lichen-patch pale, but the side that is battered by the elements – the Cailleach's worn, lined face – is honeycomb thin, warmed by moss. As I step closer, I see that the pocked surface of the stone has been scattered with treasures. There are coins, pebbles, a twist of rope, a Virgin Mary pendant, an amber necklace, a rose-pink crystal, a pencil and a pile of green sea-glass shards. A white beaded rosary hangs down across the Hag's back. I find a little stuffed zebra, interlinked rings and a snail shell – although possibly the snail lives on within it. Mum shows me a carefully crafted fae doll with a green woven dress, a ceramic carved face, beaded arms and wire-twist hair. Nasturtiums and heartsease fern grow up around the Cailleach's feet. As I lay my hand gently on the rock, intuiting her steadfastness, I feel the sun on my face, beaming through my closed eyelids. We rifle for offerings – we too would like to pay our respects to the Cailleach – and Mum gives her a shiny coin. My pockets are empty, but looking down, I notice a white quartz pebble half buried in the path. I unearth it and wash it clean with water from my water bottle, tucking the quartz into a corner behind a door key and a rusted clock-winder. When this Queen of Winter assumes her veil of fog, I hope my quartz will lend her its glow.

Later, Mum will tell me that for her, the Cailleach was the most memorable of all the places we visited together, and I will think about love and lineage; about the ways in which knowledge, truth and stories are passed down. I will remember her hair – grey now, streaked with ebony – blowing as she called to me on the clifftop, drawing me with her to the deity's side. Possessing the wisdom of both age and winter, the Cailleach is a goddess who understands weather with a depth of perception we cannot conceive. As a society that so often devalues the experiences and understanding of women in later life, we have lost much, perhaps including our connection to fog, wind and snow. If the Cailleach, as guardian of the natural world, protects its delicate balance from humanity's damages, I am not alone in needing her; this wise influence is sorely required by us all in these fragmentary, threatened times. As Mum and I turn to leave, a rust-red butterfly appears, gossamer wings flitting over the stone and away. In Irish folklore, a butterfly represents the soul of the dead – a symbol of transformation and rebirth. This is a creature that can pass through the veil from the Otherworld into our own. To me, its wings beat out a message.

The Cailleach, sometimes known by the name Boí, or Buí, is in local legend said to have lived on nearby Oileán Baoi – Dursey Island. The day after visiting her we take a trip to this island, which is accessed via Ireland's only cable car. It is windy and we are apprehensive as we step into the whitewashed interior of the cable car with its wooden benches and wide windows. Passing along wires over the churning waters of the Dursey Sound, the car sways, but only gently. Sun flickers over the ceiling in shifting patches and all around us is a searching coastal light that gilds the sea and whisks into the cable car corners. A brisk, bewitching, truthful kind of light. Alongside the island, Crow Head is visible: a headland that hosts a small plaque commemorating 23 July 1943, the day a German Luftwaffe Junkers Ju-88 bomber aircraft crashed in dense fog nearby, killing all on board. On our way to Dursey we had searched for the sign, but finding ourselves lost in narrowing lanes, turned around, anxious to catch the cable car before the wind got up. Later, I find an image online of the plaque, which lists the plane's crew: Hans Auschner, Gerhard Dummler, Johannes Kuschidlo, Bruno Noth. Like the commemorative plaque for the Severn barges, it is a poignant reminder of fog's potential for fatal danger. These four men, who were buried in Co. Wicklow, far from their homes, were brought down by the fog of the Atlantic, but they also suffered due to the fog of war.

There is no one in sight as we unhook the cable car door and step down onto the island, just a few cars presumably belonging to the handful of residents for whom the cable car (which can also be used to transport sheep or smaller cattle) is the only means of accessing the mainland bar an intermittent ferry in the warmer months. We follow the single road, passing a boathouse with lobster pots stacked outside. Below us, between road and sea, is a ruined chapel contained by a drystone wall. One of its empty windows looks out to sea, one in to shore. In its graveyard, some headstones appear to be relatively recent, but most are worn almost to disappearing, their stone gradually thinned by the lichen that spreads across the surface. The ground between the graves is so bulbous and undulating it is as if the dead beneath might be stirring. We stand looking down at the church and a small flock of sheep trots along the clifftop past the graveyard, following a desire line in the tufty grass that only they can perceive.

Behind us, a gruff exclamation in Irish, and we turn to see a man leaning out of the window of a slowly moving car: he is calling not to us but to his sheepdog, an alert border collie. We watch as the dog, calmly guided by the farmer, expertly herds the sheep around the chapel and away along the clifftop.

The church has been a ruin for hundreds of years and we find moss, ferns and the dried heads of once-pink sea thrift growing within its walls. Amid the sound of wind and waves, I catch the squeak of a red-billed chough. Like the stones we have visited, this too is a place of meaning, somewhere that in the fog would be completely haunting and possibly even feel haunted. I have long been drawn to graveyards, not so much as places of sadness, but of quiet contemplation and escape. When my eldest son was a baby, I pushed his pram daily around the Victorian cemetery that was over the wall at the end of our back garden. I admired the angels and, at a turbulent time, took comfort in leafy peace and the constancy of stone.

On a wave-battered rock between Dursey and the mainland, a group of gannets sit. Dursey Island, a sign here tells us, is the last place the sun sets in Europe: this is the location that receives the last vestiges of every day's light. It has also seen darkness, being the site of a massacre led by Queen Elizabeth I's commander George Carew in which 300 men, women and children were murdered – island inhabitants and those seeking safety in the aftermath of the Battle of Kinsale. Blood has seeped into the salted soil and the stain of it cannot be erased. Now, as choughs fly overhead, in the distance I make out one of three rocks (Cow, Bull and Calf, a trio in some local tellings created by the Cailleach) that stand at the end of the island. Calf Rock is visible, and so too are the rust-red remains of its old lighthouse, which was partially destroyed by a wave in 1881, leaving six men marooned until they were rescued two weeks later by local fishermen in rowing boats. A replacement lighthouse was built on Bull Rock, its light and fog signal established in 1889. A fog signal operated on the rock for one hundred years and the light – now automatic, like Start Point – remains today.

I have examined photographs of Bull Rock: an immense, imposing jagged outcrop with the lighthouse perched high on top. Hundreds of steps leading from the boat landing to the lighthouse tower are cut into the side of the rock face. Beneath the rock runs a natural tunnel, an archway through which tour boats pass in the summer. But Bull Rock also has another name, a darker name that speaks of death – it is known as Tech Duinn, meaning 'House of Donn'. In Irish mythology, Donn is a lonely god of the Otherworld, ruler of the dead, whom he takes to live with him in Tech Duinn, realm of the dead. The Otherworld, untethered by time or space, would sometimes appear as an island in Western seas and at other times it was said it could be reached by means of travelling through a lake or cave. So, Tech Duinn's unusual rocky sea-bound archway resembles a passing point, a portal, said to be a route by which dead souls could travel to the land of ancestors. Although I strain my eyes, I cannot see Bull Rock from where I stand now on Dursey Island, but later I will glimpse it in the distance from the mainland. It's a clear day, but the sea around Tech Duinn will be swathed in mist.

As we drive back, the mountains are layered against a scarlet sunset, molten pools of gold at their foothills. Although the sun is sinking fast, we venture through a blanket bog – the 'blanket' being a thick expanse of peat – on our way to a small harbour. The road over the bog is humped like a rollercoaster: the car travels down and up, down and up until I'm almost dizzy. The last of the light is shining on the mirror-like pools of water that lie over the bog, and in that moment I understand how lakes could be entrances to the Otherworld, and am reminded of why ancient people might have placed votive offerings into water. Annie Proulx describes water as transformative: 'the original shape-shifter'. It is also, I have come to realise, the way that I experience place. It is my means of entering into a landscape: and so, once again, in the absence of fog, I must settle for a swim.

I lower myself into the dark peaty water of Pulleen, a contained harbour fed by streams that flow through the bog, having rushed down from the mountains. Cold pulls tight against my body but the high water is silky smooth and my skin tingles with salt. The sun has sunk away below the mountain now, and the sky is melting into dark. I lie for a moment drifting in the midst of the bog, which is – like the Fens – a liminal landscape, time suspended in its peat-rich pools. I look out through the narrow mouth of the harbour at the crashing grey Atlantic Ocean, vainly searching the horizon for a peak of land emerging from a bank of fog. Somewhere in the sea off the West of Ireland, folklore tells of a mythical island called Hy-Brasil – a disappearing landmass obscured by fog. This magical place could only be seen once every seven years, when the fog cleared. It was marked as a known location on early maps, but in time began to be labelled an 'imaginary' island and then, later, as a rock, before vanishing altogether. Against reason, I hope that it is out there somewhere, secret and fog-swaddled – a fabled land to which a fog-self might one day find her way.

Bog is the domain of moss, specifically layers of carbon-storing Sphagnum, which contains both cells that photosynthesise light and cells that absorb water, thus ensuring that moss-covered bog remains damp. Beara's blanket bogs are a habitat in which moss thrives, so too is the recently restored Beara Rainforest: thirty-two acres of oak and other native tree species that are, like the oak grove of Wistman's Wood, rich in epiphytes such as moss and lichen. Robin Wall Kimmerer describes the way in which rainforest moss absorbs water, specifically fog: 'hair-like leaf points and delicate branches invite the condensation of fog droplets'. She explains that – like the blackberries I once gathered on my cemetery pram walks to make jam – moss contains pectin within its cell walls, which allows it to 'absorb water vapour directly from the atmosphere'. I do not have to experience Beara's fog to know that it belongs to this landscape – fog is here, part of the fabric of this finely balanced watery world.

The next day, to reach the Cashelkeelty stone circles (Caiseal Chaoilte) we follow an elusive path up through damp woods, gingerly crossing a stream over slippery stones and climbing through trees alongside falling water. The oak branches that hang with ferns, and the moss-covered boulders, are reminiscent of the Celtic rainforest at the base of Cadair Idris. Here too is a constant sound of splashing as the river, fed by mountain streams, dashes down wooded hillside towards the sea. The quartz-littered path through this valley is another glistening, rock-scattered winterbourne. Above us the scoop of the mountains rises, boulder-scattered and craggy. The ground is littered with silver birch leaves and banks of crisp bracken. Beside the path stands a glossy holly tree with plentiful red berries; towering above it, an electricity pylon

hums. A lone sheep stands sentinel. In between lush woodland and sheer rock face we find the stone circle. We can see
salt water – when the sun comes out, the stones cast shadows
that point to the sea. Up on the top here the wind is blustery,
wrapping my scarf around my face. A second group of stones
sits a little further down the hillside and, on a flat altar-like
stone, is a collection of offerings: shells, quartz pebbles and a
feather standing upright like a prayer flag.

The light is pristine, but softly hazy – there's a shimmer to
the air and, as a raven flies past in front of the hillside, the rocks
glint in the sun. This is a quality of light I haven't seen before.
It's at once both sunny and misty – a light that questions and
murmurs; a light that perhaps belongs uniquely to this ancient place of ritual and myth. These moss-spotted stones are
a gathering place, a viewpoint, a site outside time. They are
steady, but not static – standing among them, the air seems taut
with silent reverberation, like the sensation of stepping into a
room and seeing heads turn to look at me. 'There is,' writes
Robin Wall Kimmerer, 'an ancient conversation going on
between mosses and rocks, poetry to be sure. About light and
shadow and the drift of continents.' I have briefly interrupted
their dialogue with my presence but, as I leave, the exchange
will continue. The lines of this silently spoken poem must
also make mention of fog: the mystery of its shifting strands
slipping around constant stone; the memory of its presence
that has been imbibed and held ever close by soft, green moss.

The final stone circle of our trip – Uragh (An Iúrach) –
stands at the end of a path edged by whispering grasses that
opens out to a wide valley surrounded by peaks and untouched
by evidence of human habitation. On one side is a wooded

hillside, on the other, moorland. Following the path as it emerges out into the valley, I let out a cry of surprise. The stone circle is there directly ahead of us, majestic on a hill-ock at the centre of an expansive vista encompassing water, rock and sky; it is the focal point of the landscape. There are five stones, together with a much taller axial stone, and through them I glimpse the spreading shine of calm, beryl-blue water – Lough Inchiquin. Cascading down the hillside directly behind the stone circle, at the far end of the lough, is the Gleninchaquin Waterfall – five gushing silver streams that converge in a flowing fall. This is a mystical location; one of the most memorable vistas I have ever seen.

Later, listening back to the voice notes I record there, I hear myself palpably gasp with awe. Clouds rush endlessly by overhead, and these stones are connected to the firmament, their positioning orientated according to sun, moon and stars. This is a place where the landscape speaks – a gateway to somewhere else, or a space in which it seems possible to become someone else, a land of falling and still water, of rock, stone and air. The grass murmurs with forgotten voices – in this land out of time, I could be in any century. Feeling small, I lay the palm of my hand on the mossy axial stone to steady myself. Perhaps the whispers I hear are that age-old ceaseless conversation between moss and stone. There is no fog to be seen here, but on the hillock beneath spreading sky, I seem to sense it – fog droplets are held in the moss, buried deep in the lough and ever-moving through the waterfall. Just then, over the far hillside, yet another rainbow appears – a narrow arc pointing directly down like an arrow towards the lough.

In *Ebb and Flow* (a guide to restoring our relationship with the planet's waters), Irish writer Easky Britton writes of our innate connection to water, saying that 'we have a physical memory in our bodies of what it means to be home in water'. Born with this memory of suspension in water, we also contain water within us – human bodies consist of 60–70 per cent water. Each of us is, like fog, an ongoing participant in the water cycle. Perhaps not everyone has a fog-self, but we do all live as our water-self. Easky Britton describes also the concept of the 'memory of water', which is, she writes, 'something that was already known by Indigenous people and ancient wisdom traditions all over the world'. This is the idea, largely unacknowledged by current science, that water molecules can exhibit a memory effect. I find this a bewitching thought. Does the water below me in the darkness at the bottom of the lough remember that it was once light, floating fog? Do the clouds remember, does the rushing waterfall? A rainbow too is made up of water – droplets that reflect and separate light. When this rainbow's colours fade, perhaps the water will remember that it was once a radiant arc across the sky. I like to think that this could be so. I do know that whenever I plunge myself into water – fog, lake, quarry or sea – I carry away the memory of that moment, not just in my mind but in my body; my skin tingles with connection long after I am warm and dry.

Back at the stone cottage, I light a fire in the stove. Along the bedroom wall, a picture window faces out across the mountains, and on either side of the bed there is a skylight. The sky is cloudless and I lie in bed watching the stars. I wonder which of them were so significant for the Bronze Age people that they built their stone circles in alignment with them.

*

The next morning, our last day in Ireland, opening my eyes in the dawn light, I can see one bright star looking down into the morning. As the star fades and the sun comes up behind the mountains, the sky moves through pink and purple, orange and red, clouds spread thickly like brushstrokes. Two crows sitting on a telephone wire are silhouetted against the sunrise. I look again out of the picture window, and then I see it: white mist creeping up from the lake at the bottom of the valley. It is a low mist, coating the fields and the calmly grazing sheep with a dusty shake of icing sugar. A shape-changing mist, at the sides of the valley it drapes delicately across the fields like a wedding veil while in the centre it is denser, rising vaporous over the lake. Perhaps it is not wise to rush out and chase féth fíada, but I cannot resist. I tug my boots on over my pyjamas and throw on a coat. 'I'll be back!' I call to Mum as I hurry out the cottage door, camera in hand.

The October air is crisp, scented with bracken, wood smoke and a hint of salt. I venture along the road towards the bog. The subdued sky ripples with mackerel scales of cirrocumulus clouds, the last vestiges of sunrise seeping out from behind the rocky hilltop, a glow echoed by heads of dry grasses that carpet the bog. I can hear the sound of running water and the call of a wren, and beneath that I feel the presence of the bog, covered by peat and silence. Between the road and the hillside a polished oval pool is edged by slender reeds. Its water reflects the clouds' changing colours and the pool is bisected by light – one side dark and unfathomable, the other a luminous crescent of sky. All across the surface slender wreaths of mist waft up from the water, their constant dance the only movement in a motionless landscape. I stand and watch them shiver, as if they might at any moment solidify into human or animal form. I feel, in that moment, that the Otherworld and its mysteries are right at hand, just below the water's surface. I had hoped to find the mystic among standing stones and ancient boulders – I did not expect to find a thin place in a bog on a misty morning. Standing in quietude, I lose track of time, as the siren mist sings and the morning waits in hushed serenity. Eventually sun begins to peek above the mountain and I pull myself away from the beckoning bog to walk back, along a lane edged with mossy rocks.

The grass in the fields has been sprinkled with ice crystals – it is the first frost of the year. Mist has arrived with the winter, as if it were a gift from the Cailleach. In the valley behind the cottage, it drifts up from the lake and floats across the fields, drystone walls and yellow-dotted gorse bushes. This is the most pallid mist I've ever seen: its puffs of cloud float low to the ground, barely clearing the highest hedges and spreading like the white lace shawl my grandma knitted for me as a baby, which – years later – I wrapped around my own children. A cluster of sheep grazes in the rocky field before the lake. Like the bog pool, it reflects the softly striped sky, its water limpid with a mottling of weed on the surface. Around the sunken valley, mist clings to the fields, just out of my reach. Held back by hedge and fence, I can't get close enough to step into it, but it feels like the kind of teasing mist that would disappear as soon as I approached it – an otherworldly mist. I walk back to the cottage, where seven baby starlings sit chattering on the roof, spreading out along the telephone wire.

I have counted rainbows, stars and birds; I have communed with ancient stones, I have ventured into a moss-rich bog in search of portals that shine back sky. I found the mist that I was seeking — or could it be that the mist found me? Féth fíada is also called ceo draíochta (druids' fog): an indicator (or a by-product) of the proximity of magic — that which we sense, not see. Its presence — like the butterfly, the rainbow, the glimmering light — speaks to me as an omen. Each encounter hints at the thinness of the veil between this world and the Celtic Otherworld. Rather than obscuring my vision, ceo draíochta — the gauzy, mythical mist — is a symbol of the unseen and a reminder for me to follow my intuition and open myself up to the possibility of the unseeable. The further I have chased fog the clearer it has become that, even when I study forecasts, I can never truly predict it: my most meaningful encounters with fog occur when I release myself from the pressure to find it and accept its appearance as a blessing. To me, fog is one of the beautiful, inexplicable mysteries of the universe.

8

THE FLAVOUR OF FOG –
RIVER THAMES

(pea-souper – smog – sense of taste)

Fog everywhere. Fog up the river, where it
flows among green aits and meadows; fog
down the river, where it rolls defiled among
the tiers of shipping, and the waterside
pollutions of a great (and dirty) city. Fog on
the Essex marshes, fog on the Kentish heights.

CHARLES DICKENS, *Bleak House*

I catch the train to London from Kemble station, arriving in
the early hours. It is dark at the Victorian country station,
which has always felt to me like it belongs in the children's
story *The Box of Delights*. As I stand and wait on this wintery
November morning, I imagine wolves running through the
encroaching gloom, as a schoolboy meets a time-travelling
magician on the platform. On the train, I doze as we speed

through crepuscular countryside towards the city. Like Dickens' fog, I intend to go up the river and down the river, travelling from source to mouth, and back again. In the fields near Kemble, at Thames Head, is the source of the River Thames. From this river originates the London fog: snaking its way through London – Dickens' 'great (and dirty) city' – the Thames is situated in a low-lying basin and, like the Severn, it is prone to inversion fog. Now only a few patches of marshland remain, mostly towards the river mouth, but in Roman times much of the river basin would have been marshy – not unlike the Fens – and prone to rising mist. Although there may have been existing British settlements in the area, it was the Romans who, recognising the river's military and commercial potential, built the settlement called Londinium in a damp landscape, crossing the Thames with a timber bridge. 'The fortunes of the city,' London historian Peter Ackroyd writes in *Thames*, 'were irretrievably tied to the presence of the tidal river.' While it is a city famous for fogs, in reality, to look for fog in London is to seek the past. Dan, who grew up in London and travelled to school on the tube each day, tells me he can barely remember a foggy morning, but the previous generation of Londoners would have experienced smog – the word (a portmanteau of smoke and fog) coined to describe the city's thick, dirty fogs that were often referred to as 'pea-soupers'. My dad, born in a different industrial, smog-prone English city – Sheffield – tells me that: 'Walking to school when I was around ten, the smog was so thick you could almost taste it.'

After taking the tube from Paddington to London Bridge, I step out into grey city rain. There's an early morning gentleness – London hasn't yet woken up and acquired its sharp edges. Cloud has mellowed everything and sleepiness is in the air. Wet pavements shine and windows above shops glow orange, as the high-rise buildings of the City of London financial district are glittered by the rising sun. The Thames has long recalled to me *The Waste Land*, particularly on a winter morning. In the poem, T. S. Eliot describes a wave of morning commuters crossing London Bridge as a zombie-like passage of the dead, and refers to the foggy winter city as 'unreal'. Today, with the drizzle, it is colourful umbrellas that flow across London Bridge in a bobbing rainbow – this is a crowd that is fully alive.

I lean on the slippery parapet for my first sight of the brown river, which flows under Tower Bridge, passing the Tower of London on the far bank and, in the misty distance, winding around the skyscrapers of Canary Wharf. A Thames Clipper boat passes below the bridge in the direction of the estuary as a train clatters across the water over the Cannon Street railway bridge. Festoon lights and lanterns shine along the riverbank in front of London Bridge Hospital, the stone and white-washed facade of which abuts the river, where a scattering of leaves floats along on the water surface. Red double-decker buses and a stream of bicycles whizz behind me, across the bridge and out into the morning. A street-sweeper sits on the steps of a building, eating his breakfast. Despite the rain, cold against my cheeks, I am sleepy and my thoughts are fogged. I duck into a cafe to buy an espresso, the dark, bitter taste of which I take out into the drab dawn.

T. S. Eliot's fog was brown – smog of the early twentieth century. In *Colours of London*, Peter Ackroyd describes how the colours of this polluted fog 'altered with its changes of density when wreaths of one colour would mingle with another, getting heavier and darker as they approached the heart of the city where "misty black" gathered at the dead centre'. From Victorian times until the smog gradually faded away (in the years following the Clean Air Act of 1956), the water vapour of London's natural white fog mingled with smoke released by factories and home fires, taking on a mixture of hues from yellow to brown, and sometimes even black, when it contained sufficient soot. 'The yellow colour,' writes Christine L. Corton in *London Fog: The Biography*, 'was caused by the fog's high sulphur content.' It was this yellowness, she explains, that led to London fog being dubbed 'pea soup' by the American writer Herman Melville in 1849; at the time, pea soup tended to be made not from fresh green peas but from yellow split peas, particularly by the poor. London's pea-souper fogs were dangerous, posing a deadly threat to health through illness (particularly of the lungs) and also by increasing the risk of accident on the roads and on the river: a danger depicted by Dickens in incidents such as the fog-bound steamer collision that occurs in *Our Mutual Friend*. But the transformative effects of this thickly swirling fog appealed to the public imagination: London fog, preserved in literature and art, became so much an integral part of the character of the city that London's foggy associations endure today.

Oscar Wilde, in his essay 'The Decay of Lying', refers to 'those wonderful brown fogs that come creeping down our streets, blurring the gas-lamps' – fogs he attributes to the Impressionists. He is believed to have been referring particularly to American artist James McNeill Whistler, who painted a foggy series of *London Nocturnes* and who said – explaining his inspiration for the series in his 'Ten O'Clock Lecture' (a public lecture on art given in 1885 in Piccadilly) – that 'the evening mist clothes the riverside with poetry, as with a veil'. Wilde too saw the poetry in mist – he maintained that: 'People see fogs, not because there are fogs, but because poets and painters have taught them the mysterious loveliness of such effects.' I scratch around in the corners of my mind, trying to recall wisps of fog that could have clung from my own studies of poetry. 'One does not see anything until one sees its beauty,' Wilde wrote, and for me this has certainly been true of fog. No longer just weather to me, over time fog has revealed both loveliness and meaning.

For poets and painters to have taught us to see fog, there must have been something in fog as a subject that called to them – a secret sparkle reflecting their unique and particular visions. Seeing in this visionary way is a creative gift; perhaps poets and painters have an instinctive understanding of the paradoxical way that fog can simultaneously conceal, create and reveal beauty. Sometimes when I go chasing fog, what I am actually chasing is a half-remembered image of it. In the case of London, I am (perhaps fruitlessly) pursing a black and white photograph I once saw in which a winter morning fog was subsuming the river, the Houses of Parliament emerging from cloud in the background. This is the London I seek, but it's also an iconic view that is immediately familiar, having been immortalised by a key Impressionist figure: Claude Monet. He, like Whistler, was a painter who, as an outsider, viewed the London fog with fresh, unclouded eyes.

Last year, on a visit to Paris with my family, I unexpectedly came across one of Monet's London paintings in the Musée d'Orsay: *London Houses of Parliament, The Sun Shining through the Fog*. Crowds were gathered by *Water Lilies* nearby, but in front of *The Sun Shining through the Fog*, there was ample space for me to stand alone and look. The painting portrays the Houses of Parliament during a dreamlike foggy sunset, more vibrant than any I have seen. In the low light of the sun, the fog shines purple, red and gold, sky mirrored by river water. The painting's colours are almost garish, but its lines and shapes have been blurred by fog. The scene depicted felt unnatural to me, even a little apocalyptic, but there was joy in it, too. Monet, who worked on his oil sketches of the Houses of Parliament from a terrace at St Thomas' Hospital opposite, wrote to his wife Alice (four years before this particular painting was completed): 'Yesterday there was sun, with an exquisite mist and a splendid sunset.' Monet's love for fog glows out from the canvas – in his work, the smudging, smoky atmospheric effects of smog are elevated to the sublime. He is quoted as saying that: 'Without the fog, London would not be a beautiful city. It is the fog that gives it its marvellous breadth.'

I step into the National Gallery to see one of Monet's earlier misty works: *The Thames below Westminster*, another painting in which the Houses of Parliament and Westminster Bridge fade into a haze of fog. At the foreground is a wooden jetty where shadowy figures work above the river. Tug-boats send up smoke from their chimneys, blending into the fog. On the Embankment is a row of trees with figures grouped below them – this part of the scene not unlike my walk alongside the river earlier in the day. I can differentiate daubs on the canvas, a visible texture where the paint catches the light. In this shadowy, soothing scene, the colours are primrose, grey and peach, the sky an echo of the brushstroke-clear river. The spires of the Houses of Parliament appear dreamy and fantastical – it is the Thames workmen, the ladder and the jetty (its shadow fractured by the river) that have the most clarity and give the painting structure. On my way out of the gallery, the glass atrium dome casts gentle light over a Turner painting – *Sun Rising through Vapour.* In this scene, with its *contre-jour* lighting (lit from behind the subject), fishermen are at work in sea mist, the sun's reflection in the water is milky, the sky is aureate. Turner, like Monet, also painted London's fog, notably in *The Thames above Waterloo Bridge*, a creamy, dreamlike scene in which two steamboats churn billowing smoke that blends into the smoggy air.

In heading to the mouth of the river, I will follow in the footsteps of Turner, whose *Mouth of the Thames Sketchbook* depicted 'waterside terrain including shipping and riverbanks' in Essex and Kent, on either side of the Thames not far from where it meets the sea. One location specifically mentioned in this sketchbook is Purfleet in Essex, an estuary town that adjoins Rainham Marshes. In *Heart of Darkness*, Joseph Conrad described the mist on the Essex estuary marshes as being 'like a gauzy and radiant fabric, hung from the wooded rises inland, and draping the low shores in diaphanous folds'. Conrad's literary technique here has been described as Impressionist. He, like Monet, closely observed the atmospheric changes created by mist, noting its effect on the sky, which he called 'a benign immensity of unstained light'. The phenomenon evoked is delicate and sheer, like the bleached plumes rising from the mist-mantled Fens – a natural sight in contrast with the thick, polluted smog of the city – but the novel's protagonist, Marlow, refers to this stretch of the Thames as 'the very end of the world, a sea the colour of lead, a sky the colour of smoke'. He pictures a Roman military camp 'lost in a wilderness, like a needle in a bundle of hay – cold, fog, tempests, disease, exile and death'. The estuarine river has been, he proclaims, 'one of the dark places of the earth'. In this vision, Thames fog is a source not of beauty, but of hopeless cold and damp disease, the river having exacted a terrible price from the Romans for their infraction.

Hoping to catch a glimpse of mist over the marshes, I catch a train from central London out to Purfleet. Trains thunder past on the other line and a crow flies overhead (perhaps searching for actualities). We pass allotments, neat back gardens and tangled banks of brambles. The sky is uniform grey, the carriage windows decorated with droplets. Moving through a flat landscape of pylons and ponies, factories and flyovers, the train runs parallel with the Thames. Unlike the city river, this stretch feels untamed. It's a breezy day when I reach Purfleet and the greyscale water is choppy, swiping my face and filling my nose, the taste of salt scraping at the back of my throat. A tug-boat passes, leading an immense tanker into a port – probably Tilbury – further along the estuary, and another Thames Clipper passes it quickly in the opposite direction, heading back to the city. In the rainy distance, cars beetle across the Queen Elizabeth II Bridge – also known as the Dartford Crossing – and I walk the empty path on the edge of town towards Rainham Marshes. Down on the foreshore

are the partially submerged remains of a Neolithic forest –
these trees even older than the petrified stumps that emerged
from the sea in Aberdyfi. The river, a rippling brown velvet
ribbon, rushes on alongside the marsh edged by long grasses
that swish in the wind. On the opposite bank I spot the square
yellow outline of what appears to be a navigational light like
the one beside the lighthouse keeper's cottage on the Severn,
although the river here is wide and visibility is low, so without
binoculars it's difficult to be sure.

I cross a bridge over a small stream to RSPB Rainham
Marshes. Alongside the path, a row of hawthorn bushes with
dwindling red haws and fading foliage. A sign here describes
the Thames as 'a liquid heritage and an iconic landscape',
home to a variety of plants, insects and animals – plus half
a million migrating birds – but, it notes, the marshes and
mudflats are under threat from the changing climate, and
rising sea levels will inevitably affect the shape of this estuary.
A group of schoolchildren walk past me, carrying clipboards
and chattering excitedly. They bustle into the nature reserve,
boots on and hair tucked under woolly hats, battling the
wind. In the cafe, I order a cup of tea and a cheese toastie,
which I eat sitting beside a long window that looks out onto
the marsh. I watch the caterpillar of children twist errati-
cally along a path parallel to a dyke, heading deeper into the
reserve. Beyond them on the horizon, wind turbines turn,
the spindly forms of pylons stand in parallel rows, and a road
runs high over the marsh across a flyover. Human habitation
and industrial development close by surround this small,
protected reserve, where silver pools of unshaken water – on
which birds huddle – echo clouded sky. Like the Fens and

the blanket bog, this ancient marshland is low and level, a tiny remaining pocket of the wetlands that were once here, spreading and mist-prone.

As I walk back, the keen wind wails and the skeletal remains of brittle umbellifers lean away from it. On a far bend of the river, almost hidden by low cloud, I can see the towers of Canary Wharf, but before returning to the city I stop by St Stephen's Church, where a green plaque affixed to a flint wall notes Purfleet's association with a literary character who could direct fog to his will: Bram Stoker's Dracula. The plaque reads: 'Dracula moves to Carfax House at Purfleet on a by-road to London. Probably based on Purfleet House, built by Samuel Whitbread, now the site of St Stephen's Church.' In the book, Dracula first comes to England on a merchant ship called the *Demeter*, which reaches shore at Whitby – a dead man lashed to the helm – in a dense sea fog: 'White, wet clouds, which swept by in ghostly fashion, so dank and damp and cold that it needed but little effort of imagination to think that the spirits of those lost at sea were touching their living brethren with the clammy hands of death.' Later, when the men have gone to Purfleet to look for Dracula at Carfax, Mina Harker writes in her diary of 'a thin streak of white mist, that crept with almost imperceptible slowness across the grass towards the house, seemed to have a sentience and a vitality of its own'. In what she assumes to be a dream, Mina witnesses this mist become dense fog as it enters the house and takes on something close to human form: 'It got thicker and thicker, till it seemed as if it became concentrated into a sort of pillar of cloud in the room.' There is a red glow that at first she takes to be the gaslight, but which then, she writes, 'seemed to shine on me through the fog like two red eyes'. The vampire, in fog form, has infiltrated the home.

Stoker's descriptions are fog at its most chilling and gothic – the creeping disguise of a harbinger of death, the vampire's red eyes reflecting his taste for blood. In *Estuary*, her intimate exploration of the Thames Estuary, Rachel Lichtenstein quotes a conversation with writer Iain Sinclair in which he notes the metaphorical parallel between the mythology of Dracula, who 'distributes coffins of Transylvanian earth' from Purfleet, and the town's current existence as 'a distribution centre for oil and petrol'. The oil industry exists as a threat to the town, to the river, and to all that lies beyond – even the fog. Through blood and oil, a shade of the darkness once attached to this part of the river lingers, and on a dull winter day its gloom is easily felt. Yet the melancholy estuary can also be seen as, Peter Ackroyd writes, 'a place of mystery and of enchantment'. The river marshes with their wavering light are, like the Fens, a changeable combination of water and land, where salt and spreading skies cast a subtle spell. Walking in the solitary marshes, setting my face against the wind as I passed the submerged stumps of long-dead trees, I did feel a sense of gathering strangeness; I was suddenly aware of the river as a primeval force.

On the train back to London, I recall my past experiences of the Thames, remembering the days when my children were smaller and, visiting their grandparents in the city, we would walk along the Southbank at low tide, eyes to the mud in search of flotsam from the river. Close to the ground and clear-eyed, the boys spotted sea glass, pottery shards and countless white clay pipes – once as ubiquitous as cigarette butts – slender pieces of the past that they could roll between their fingers, a tangible connection to the story of the city. Now, in order to protect the historical integrity of the Thames foreshore, it's no longer possible even to pick up items from the beach surface without a permit, so mudlarking is the preserve of the few. Lara Maiklem – a mudlarker for almost twenty years, and author of the book *Mudlarking: Lost and Found on the River Thames* – describes her experience mudlarking alongside the river as a fog rolls in and time seems to stand still, saying that: 'The spirits of the foreshore rise up in the mist, just out of sight.' She pictures figures from various moments in the river's past going about their business, concealed by 'swirling whiteness'. In my own mind, the river mist could hide spirits from as far back in time as those Roman soldiers crossing the waters on a wooden bridge, perhaps watched from a distance by Iceni in the shadows. Lara Maiklem calls Thames fogs 'quite literally the mists of time', and if all evidence of our current century vanished into the fog I would not find it at all difficult to believe that the river could summon spirits of the past.

In exploring the Thames Marshes, Rachel Lichtenstein describes meeting a local historian and mudlarker called River Jim who found items out in the marshes that reflect their many layers of history, including Victorian objects, Roman pottery, and flints from Doggerland– the landmass that once connected Britain to Continental Europe, incorporating both the Thames Basin and the East Anglian Fens. It was historical climate change that caused Doggerland to be slowly enveloped by what we now call the North Sea, following a glacial melt around 6500 BCE. Annie Proulx imagines that time when 'there were fogs and the cries of frogs and waterbirds, the sky-darkening skeins of migratory flights, the steady upward creep of chill seawater'. Only a few flinty fragments of that lost and buried landscape now endure, preserved in peat. It is their peat-rich nature that makes the salt marshes highly effective carbon sinks – they could be a crucial defence against current climate change. Were they to be allowed, these marshes would spread and return to their watery ways, as if remembering those misty days of pre-Roman times when untouched wetlands covered the river basin.

As Conrad suggested, the Romans – accustomed to warmer climes – would almost certainly not have enjoyed the inhospitable, damp situation in which they found themselves. Roman civil servant and historian Herodian wrote of Britain that 'because of the thick mist which rises from the marshes, the atmosphere in this region is always gloomy'. In that time, which seems impossibly long ago, Londonium was razed by the Iceni under Boudicca (whose territory included parts of Fenland and who, growing up in East Anglia, was something of a heroine to me in my teens). It was rebuilt before finally being abandoned around 450 CE and, remarkably, a fragment of its surrounding wall stands on Tower Hill not far from Fenchurch Street station, where I alight from the Purfleet train. Once six metres high, the wall fell into disrepair when Londinium was deserted, but it was mended and heightened in the medieval period and stripes of red brickwork run through the original Roman part of the wall. In front is a bronze sculpture believed to be of the emperor Trajan. Wearing a tunic, he is not dressed for the English winter. I stand beside him in my wool scarf and waterproof mac, as raindrops fall on his bare arms and time twists around us.

'London,' A. A. Gill wrote, 'is a city of ghosts; you feel them here.' Out in the marshes the layers of history are buried, but in London they are ever-present, woven through the fabric of the city. At the city's core is its river; flowing through the middle of London, the Thames has swallowed up countless pieces of debris that have in time become historical artefacts. Intermittently, perhaps not liking the taste, it spits them out again onto the foreshore for the mudlarks to find.

Out on the lonely marshes I felt exposed, but in the crowded heart of the city, I can disappear – I pull up my raincoat hood and blend into the stream of pedestrians that flows away from the river towards shiny-faced skyscrapers. At 22 Bishopsgate, which bills itself as the tallest building in the City of London, I take the lift up, up, and up to the viewing platform at the top. My hope had been for an aerial view of the river, but what I find, in the most unexpected of places, is fog. Cloud is so low that the skyscraper has become snagged and I am inside it. At this height the city appears dimmed by fog – all its colours faded to a palette of slate, ash and gunmetal. Rooftops and roads below form a complex, tessellated pattern, bisected by the smooth, dun sweep of the Thames. Hidden courtyards and rooftop gardens are revealed from my vantage point in the sky. The light up here on the viewing platform is flat and muted – the light of a walk in the fog, or of flying high inside a cloud.

People in the room behind me are reflected in the glass, and between outlines of window frames shadows walk out into the sky, their spectral forms hovering above the city. Raindrops trace diagonally down the tower's window-glass, flowing from cloud to ground. Through the diamond-smattered pane I see London Bridge below me, tiny red buses rolling across like my sons' now-discarded toys, people long-legged ants. Trains shudder past, silver in the gloom. 'Look at the river!' says the man standing next to me. 'It turns you around seeing it from up here – my sense of direction's gone to pot!' When I get my own bearings, on the corner of the riverbend I see once again (and now from the other direction) that cluster of tall buildings at Canary Wharf. The Thames is twisting through the city, turning left and then right, before disappearing into the distance where the marshes lie just beyond the horizon. From the river came the city; from the river came the fog.

In her introduction to the anthology *Into the London Fog: Eerie Tales from the Weird City*, editor Elizabeth Dearnley emphasises the uncanny nature of London fog: 'Recasting ordinary streets in a ghostly twilight haze, fog can make London feel both familiar and unfamiliar.' Included in this collection is Virginia Woolf's essay 'Street Haunting', in which a walk through winter streets reflects the hypnotic strangeness of the dark city. Woolf describes 'floating islands of pale light' under street lamps – passing through them, ordinary pedestrians 'wear a certain look of unreality'. A myriad of apparitions jostle the pavements of her city, one of which is the observing street haunter herself. The anonymity of London streets, particularly when cloaked in darkness, offers the walker an opportunity to observe both internal and external worlds, and for Woolf the streets represented a kind of freedom. Beside the River Thames – 'wide, mournful, peaceful' – the narrator of 'Street Haunting' receives a glimpse of the shade of her past self. Neither she nor the ever-flowing river has remained as they were in that moment – self being as mutable as water. Now, as I leave the skyscraper and walk back towards the river, I too dissolve into the crowd. The river in this haunted city whispers its stories to me but I seek water that is suspended in air – only in the fog do I feel intensely real, my fog-self slipping out silently under a shrouded sky.

In the garden of ruined church St Dunstan-in-the-East, I sit on a bench to eat a sandwich and warm my hands on another cup of coffee, having searched nearby cafes in vain for a 'London Fog' (a sugary, creamy Earl Grey-based drink). To me, though, the taste of fog would be sharp and fresh, not sweet. St Dunstan is a place of repose in a whirling city, its walls draped with hanging vines, its roofless centre open to the sky. A robin sings gaily from the top of a tree, variegated ivy growing up around its trunk. 'London Ivy' was once another term for the local fog, a phrase perpetuated by Dickens' usage in *Bleak House*: an appropriate description for a close-clinging poison.

Now, winter air drifts through extant windows, and the mottled, soot-stained walls touched by centuries of London fogs keep counsel on the secrets of the city. I am alone and the ruin feels otherworldly: Gothic archways lead to hidden steps, and the air within the walls undulates with imperceptible presence. A church was first built on this site in Saxon times and, following the Great Fire of London, it was rebuilt by Sir Christopher Wren, only to be severely damaged in the Blitz – finally becoming a public garden in the 1960s. Unlike the coloured glass of St Arilda's, the many high, arched windows of this church contain nothing but empty air. I pause for a moment in this peaceful garden just a street away from the river and watch leaves drift down onto the cobbles. Soaked in centuries of significance, St Dunstan-in-the-East – with its slow surrender of architecture to the elements, and a dimmed distinction between inside and outside – is the thinnest place I have found in this city.

London fog was not confined to the streets – at the peak of the pea-soupers, fog was so tenacious it made its way into Londoners' houses, mingling with smoke from their home fires. Marie Belloc Lowde's short story 'The Lodger' – later a novel adapted by Alfred Hitchcock into his silent chiller of the same name (subtitled 'A Story of the London Fog') – links fog's cold miasma to the presence of a mysterious (and very possibly murderous) lodger. Mrs Bunting, the landlady, listens to this man moving stealthily through her 'dark, fog-filled hall', and after he has used her kitchen for what she suspects to be the burning of (presumably bloodstained) clothes, she enters to find it 'full of fog'. So unsettled is she that, for the first time ever, she makes breakfast for herself and her husband upstairs in their bedroom: 'I couldn't stay down there,' she said, 'it was so cold and foggy.'

In this story, as in *Dracula*, the presence of interior fog indicates the proximity of an evil that has infiltrated the home. Unlike the evanescent white country fog that whispers beguilingly through my little loft-room window, the city fog was cloying and sullied by soot. In Dickens' novels too, fog could cross the divide between outside and inside, making its way into the counting-house of Scrooge in *A Christmas Carol*: 'the fog came pouring in at every chink and keyhole'. Muddled and misguided, blind to the realities of the world around him, Scrooge is a soul so lost that fog can creep in to surround him in his place of work. But at the end of the novel, a different man, he opens his window on Christmas morning and finds 'no fog, no mist' – the skies, and his eyes, have cleared, leaving nothing but 'sweet fresh air'.

Between the pages of my notebook I have slipped a postcard reproduction of a 1927 London Underground poster that reads: 'Cold rain & fog on the top abound, descend to bright-ness underground. It is warmer below.' Now, thrusting hands into coat pockets, I make my way down the piano-key steps of the tube and I take the Elizabeth line to Canary Wharf. The offices I have seen from up and down the river were built on a city peninsula cradled in the crook of the river, an area called the Isle of Dogs, the Thames flowing past three of its sides. Dickens described it as a 'low, level, marshy field, fringed with factories and taverns'. The damp marshlands were drained to make way for new docks, but this area later found itself at the heart of the Great Smog of London, a severe air-pollution event that lasted for several days in December 1952. A meteorological cold front had settled on London, bringing natural fog, and as the city's inhabitants stoked their fires to keep themselves warm they released copious chimney fumes into the unmoving foggy air, suffocating London with an all-encompassing smoke-laden yellow smog that killed thousands. It was reported that on the Isle of Dogs visibility sank to zero – fog there had become so thick that inhabitants could not even see their own feet. The horror of this 1952 Great Smog and its fatal consequences were what eventually led to the Clean Air Act of 1956, which was the beginning of the end for the London Smog.

Today at Canary Wharf, buildings – multiplying clouds in their mirrored windows – tower above the river winding below. In the Museum of London Docklands, I learn about frost fairs, which were regularly held on the frozen River Thames from as early as 695 CE, mostly between Westminster and London Bridge. Extremely low temperatures, combined with fog and snow, could produce enduring deep ice on the river. In the winter of 1434–5, the Thames was frozen so solid that people were able to walk along the ice all the way from London Bridge to Purfleet and beyond. Between the sixteenth and nineteenth centuries, seven major frost fairs were held, during which the river would become populated by booths selling food and drink to crowds who enjoyed carriage rides, skittles and swings, as well as varied entertainments. Those who usually worked as watermen and lightermen managed the ice and hired out their vessels as stages. Printing presses were even erected on the ice in order to produce and sell souvenirs. The fairs were not without danger, however – the ice could thaw quickly and unexpectedly give way.

The last frost fair, held in the winter of 1814, was so expansive that a pedestrian passageway was marked out onto the river surface. Preceding this, in December 1813 there had been an intensely cold freezing fog that 'for its density and duration has seldom been equalled,' wrote George Davis in his book *Frostiana: Or a History of the River Thames in a Frozen State*, published the year of the fair. Describing it as 'tremendous fog, or "darkness that might be *felt*"', he considered that 'the state of the metropolis, in consequence of the increased fog, was, at night, truly alarming'. Fog compounded darkness and he wrote that people were 'unavoidably compelled to carry torches' because streetlamps had been rendered useless, as they 'appeared through the haze no bigger than small candles'. Carriages collided and were overturned, and women, he felt, were particularly at risk: 'Females who had ventured abroad before the fog came on, were placed under great peril; several missed their way.' After the fog, there came heavy snow, and by February 1814 the river had become sufficiently frozen to facilitate the frost fair, which lasted for almost a week until rain began to fall. 'This fairy frost work, was soon to be dissolved,' bemoaned George Davis, 'and was doomed to vanish.' Vanish it did – that was the last Thames frost fair ever held.

In making my way back to London Bridge I will finally travel on the river, waiting at the end of the day to catch the Thames Clipper boat from Canary Wharf pier. The declining winter sun strokes the surface of the water, burnished waves rippling. A little way downriver, on the far bank at Deptford, is a wharf that used to be known as 'Deadman's Dock' because its situation on the bottom of the river curve meant that bodies frequently washed ashore. In the dangerous days of the London Ivy, any poor unfortunate lost to an accident on the fog-bound Thames might well have ended up there. Now, though, fog is infrequent and the shape of the river is deemed so unthreatening as to be decorative – a reproduction of its u-bend, rendered in brass, can be bought as a necklace from the museum shop. My boat approaches, and the clouds are silver, gulls wheeling in the day's diminishing light. The Thames Clipper's progress upriver is swift – flag on the bow stiff in the wind. The river carries me lightly, floating me far above the many layers of time buried in its depths. I am making my way back to the source, but the once-foggy Thames and its submerged secrets will keep on flowing, past Deadman's Dock to Purfleet, and all the way out to sea.

A few weeks later, I take my family to find the source of the River Thames. It's a day of smudged edges: the far fields are faded, and it's so foggy in the distance that as the car reaches the top of the escarpment, the River Severn – usually clearly discernible where it traces the horizon – is invisible, lost to cloud. We park in a litter-scattered lay-by, which does not seem an auspicious place to begin a search for what was once thought of as a sanctuary: 'the boundary between the visible and invisible realms'. In a field behind us we can see the baby river – a thin silver ribbon – twisting across a field, but to locate the source we must cross over the road and follow the Ordnance Survey map, tracing a path upwards through a dormant field. The ploughed soil, crispy with stalks of long-harvested wheat, is littered with limestone lumps that we eye in hope of fossils. My boys run ahead, over the crest of a slight hill and up into winter sky. We find the river's source in a grassy field called Trewsbury Mead, edged by drystone walls, where the air smells marshy and oxygenated. The spring-head is a sunken, circular tower of rocks – like a submerged cairn – from which clear water bubbles up. Long ago, this sacred spring would probably have been another location that attracted votive offerings, and for centuries a stone has stood here, marking the source. Until recently it stood below a huge old ash (a tree held by druids to be sacred, with the power to connect the inner self to the outer world) but the tree has gone, presumably lost to ash dieback. 'This stone was placed here to mark the source of the River Thames', the current marker reads.

I expected little of this place, but there is a compelling witchery to this water that rises, unbidden, from dark earth. Behind the source is a mound now called Trewsbury Castle, which was once a Roman camp; just as they were drawn to the power of the River Thames at its mouth, so too it seems that the Romans were compelled to seek the spring at its source. On the slope grows an ancient spindle tree, a handful of red flowers remaining on its branches, its trunk utterly entwined in ivy – another of fog's etymological echoes. In a dry season, the waters here would remain underground, but today they spread out into Trewsbury Mead, flooding the surface and following the slight downward slope of the field. My smallest boy, wearing wellies, splashes in the spring, delighted, running ahead as we trace the flow.

Beneath the surface of the incipient river, long grass leans like weed, as water flows gently in the eventual direction of the sea. I stand at its centre, the shadow of my reflection wavering. Gradually gathering strength, water pools at the bottom of the valley. There are gulls here on the flood-formed lake and I find feathers in the grass. As we approach, birds take to the air in a cloud. My smallest boy walks out into the middle of the lake – it's deep and the water goes over the top of his boots. Following a trail of scattered scarlet haws, we pass through a gate, across the road and back to the lay-by. In a tree beside the car, chaffinches sing. This is a road that I have driven many times in dense fog, not glimpsing the magical beginning of a mighty river just over the brow of the hill. Water begets water, and this hidden wellspring of the River Thames is also in a sense the source of the many incarnations of London fog. The spring, like the fog, is mysterious, its more-than-human origins outside of our control.

9

TRANSFORMED BY THE FOG – VENICE, ITALY

(calìgo – evaporation fog – sensory delight)

I watch the moon from the top-deck window of the swaying TGV train as I cross from France to Germany; it is waxing gibbous, dancing out from behind the clouds and disappearing again. I think of my toddler son, strapped in his pushchair on his first visit to Paris, hiding his beaming face in his hands and peeping out over and over, giggling with delight. Today that boy is almost sixteen: he was in school back in England as I passed though Paris, stopping for lunch. There was Kir and *mousse au chocolat*; an embroidered tablecloth; a sprinkling of green and gold leaves floating on the surface of the Canal Saint-Martin. For supper, it's a snack on the platform in Stuttgart, where I board the sleeper to Venice – my final and furthest fog-chasing destination. My dad is accompanying me on this trip: he who adores canals and elegant buildings but has never yet been to the city constructed of both, a city that dazzles all the senses, a city famous for its fog. In Venice, fog is so nuanced that Venetians have multiple words for it,

names to reflect its subtleties: *nebbia, nebbietta, foschia, calìgo . . .*
I have been to Venice both in the summer and in the winter
and I have yet to experience its fog, but this is November:
the weather forecast looks promising and I am hopeful that
in Venice I will find fog and I will somehow be remade by it.

On my first visit to Venice I came by train. I was twenty-two
years old and I arrived in burning sun – streets crowded and
canals humming. I stepped out onto the bridge opposite the railway station with the man who was to become my husband and I
fell immediately and irretrievably in love with the dream-dusted
city. The days Dan and I spent there together that summer
became a treasure I held close, occasionally drawing them out to
marvel over. It was sixteen years before we were able to return.
On a February morning in 2019 we went back to Venice; it
was my birthday and then, as now, I was wishing for fog. We
stopped at a tiny cafe in the Campo Santa Margherita, the sign
on its red facade reading simply '*Caffe*'. On the bar was a glass
case filled with *cornetti*, and behind it a curvaceous brass coffee
machine with a metallic eagle perched on top. Pigeons period-
ically fluttered in from the sunny square, flew once around and
out again. We sipped macchiatos on the window seat and ate
buttery pastries clutched in paper napkins as morning sunlight
collected around us. Over three days the fog never came, but
the city kept us close. On hearing we had visited many years
previously, more than one Venetian exclaimed, 'Ahhh, but
Venice, she does not change.' Venice, a fading belle, clutches
her fur coat close around her (as glamorous Venetian ladies do
in the wintertime) and touches her elegantly coiffured hair – the
gentle marks of time only adding to her eternal beauty.

Ensconced on the night train, I sit on my bed and read *Venice*

Revealed, a book I found on my Great Uncle Denis's bookshelf after he died. We never spoke of the city, but he – I discovered too late – had loved it as I do. Lights rush past outside the window: a riverboat, a circus, a stadium. In the sleeping compartment the pillowcases are purple gingham. My top bunk lilts with the movement of the train: sometimes a gentle cradle-rocking, sometimes a wild careering around corners. Germany recedes and the train mutters and shakes, spinning through the night, roaring like a creature loose on the rails. I am sleepy from the miniature bottle of chilled wine that was delivered to my door as a nightcap, and I switch off the light, surrendering myself to night's inky ocean, riding its waves into fitful sleep. When I wake, the light is soft and the sky outside the window is inky-blue and peach-edged – I see my shadow looking back at me from the glass. Trees are silhouetted on the horizon and low mist rises from the fields, drifting and swelling across flat countryside. Breakfast arrives on a tray: the blessed scent of coffee, a bircher yoghurt, a perfect bread roll. As I eat, I watch Italy materialise out of the morning: across the dawn distance are mountains touched by the rising sun. Soon, the train trundles out onto the causeway crossing the Venetian Lagoon and towers appear on the horizon beneath flat clouds; water glints below and seabirds fly overhead. In a vision of bell towers, palazzos and arched windows, Venice rises up out of the sea.

Perhaps Venice has not changed, but I know myself to be different to the blithe girl who first set foot in the city's streets two decades ago, different even to the woman who happily spent her birthday here, not knowing the world would become utterly unfamiliar less than a year later. Now, as I step off the train at Venice Santa Lucia, I carry those past selves cocooned within me like nesting dolls. I walk out into the winter sunshine, my rucksack overflowing with books, my mind with questions. I am here looking for fog, for transformation, and for the utterly intangible – my fog-self. Venice is a city of mystery and of the endless unexpected, a place more questions than answers. Even without fog's potential for confusion, this is somewhere I am likely to get lost rather than to be found. Winding *calli* and sudden dead ends that lead to shivering waters can be more disorientating even than moor, mountain or marsh. Just as I surrender to the fog, so too do I surrender to the unknowability of this city – her dazzling beauty, her masked secrets, her lustrous fluidity. For Venice is, as she has always been, a city of water.

Joseph Brodsky said in *Watermark: An Essay on Venice* that 'water is the image of time'. As someone who regularly throws myself into bodies of water, I wonder if I crave cold water because it reflects and represents strange, unknowable time. Although I do not understand it, I find myself preoccupied by time, and perhaps I submerge myself in its watery equivalent for this reason. Now I carry the past with me into the city of water, in hope of answers about the future. In this city, Brodsky suggests, space's answer to time is beauty – a beauty surrounded by, and carried on, water. He wrote that 'the upright lace of Venetian facades is the best line time-alias-water has left on terra firma anywhere'. If water is time, then to me this explains how fog – a cloud of water droplets that alters city and self – can be the mists of time made manifest.

We take a vaporetto ferry around the outside edge to Castello, catching the city in fragments: a stone Madonna; light on white walls; blue-green water; paint-peeled balconies; a rainbow dancing in the spray. We are staying in a small apartment in a palazzo, reached via a contained garden that leads to an entranceway scented with incense, salt and stone. Beside a staircase, the edge of the plaster peels back to reveal a fragment of mural – an ornately painted face surrounded by leafy curlicues. We pass through an arched doorway with a heavy wooden door into an inner courtyard flanked by three storeys of green-shuttered windows, plants on windowsills and a higgledy-piggledy network of pipes running up the walls. In the corner is a marble relief plaque of the winged lion of Venice, symbol of the city, a creature that adorned the trains we passed arriving into the station. I hear water rushing down the pipes and the flow of conversation through open windows. Sky spreads above, and lines of laundry stretch from wall to wall: today, in the water city, it's a drying day. Inside, the apartment opens out onto a rio – a narrow canal barely wide enough for two boats to pass. The water is so clear I see a shoal of tiny fish swimming in the direction of the sea. Reflected in the canal, morning sun anoints the tops of the opposite buildings. A boat passes, the driver whistling. In its wake, underwater buildings shiver and dance. Into the eventual stillness, a flash of blue flies fast and low down the canal – a bird so quick that I cannot identify it, and so unlikely that I afterwards wonder if perhaps I dreamt it.

In this city of the water element, everything exists twice – once in actuality and once as reflection. On a calm, clear day, Venice's canals contain a perfect, vibrating image of the buildings' lacy facades: an uncanny double of the true city that swirls away in an instant whenever a boat passes, churning the surface. The canals are not stagnant – these are living, tidal waters that rise and fall with the sea, and shift with the moon. In winter there is an ongoing risk of *acqua alta* (high water) – the peak of astronomical high tide compounded by wind and lowering atmospheric pressure. In the event of a serious *acqua alta*, sirens warn residents of impending flooding, triggering the shuttering of buildings and the laying of *passerelle* (planks) like tightropes along the streets. Exacerbated by climate change – including rising sea levels and sinking ground levels – incidences of *acqua alta* have become increasingly frequent in recent years. One way to note the marks of these progressively high sea levels is to pay attention to a prosaic feature of Venice's urban spaces: the water staircase. Sets of low steps, which occur throughout the city, 'represent the bridge between human spaces, the canal water's surface and the underwater world', and a study of their resident organisms (such as algae and clams) can provide information about ongoing changes in the waters of the lagoon. Occupying a hinterland between urban heights and pellucid depths, the staircases are pockets of liminal space.

Fog is also a factor in Venice's watery world – intermittent envelopment in fog leaves a layer of residual dampness in the air, and the shining wet stone in fog's wake is another type of mirror that can reflect and multiply the city, making it anew. But out beyond the city walls, on the island-dotted lagoon, fog can be dangerous if boats become subsumed. A few streets back from our apartment is Fondamente Nove, a quayside street where city meets lagoon. Legend tells that during nights of November fog, a floating casket can sometimes be glimpsed here, in the waters where ferry boats leave for the islands. It is a place of unsettled rest for a little girl called Guiseppina Gabriel Carmelo, who died here in a heavy fog on 29 November 1904, when the gondola in which she was travelling back to her home on the island of Murano from Venice collided with a vaparetto ferry that had unexpectedly turned back to escape the worsening, disorientating fog. Five women were lost to the lagoon that night but only the sunken body of Guiseppina, the youngest, was never recovered. Stolen and changed by the fog, she became a spectral self. It is said that her floating casket is lit by candles so that passing boats can see it – the flames an eerie portent only ever glimpsed through the fog.

Directly opposite Fondamente Nove are the red brick walls and elegant arches of San Michele, 'island of the dead' – Venice's cemetery – clearly visible across the channel. This is where Venetians and some visitors (including Joseph Brodsky) have, for centuries, been buried. In *Venice*, Jan Morris describes the foggy spectacle of a winter funeral: 'The death-boat chugs away through the mist down the Grand Canal, with a glimpse of flowers and a little train of mourning gondolas.' Eventually, the procession of boats fades into the fog as they 'disappear slowly into the distance, across the last canal'. Along the route to San Michele, funeral processions would pass an imposing, solitary pink building, poised on a corner and abutting the lagoon on two of its square sides. The Casino degli Spiriti (house of the spirits) is a palazzo with a dark and murderous past. It is said to be haunted, with reports of strange echoes, spooky figures and, perhaps more fancifully, hooded, torch-lit processions on foggy nights. Venice, like London, is a city of ghosts; the dead are never far from mind in these timeless streets and the past feels eerily present, particularly on a foggy night. In fog, the city is remoulded and time becomes fluid. Paolo Barbaro puts it so: 'It's evening, it's foggy, the night's about to end – as places and ages merge.'

Today the sky is clear, but the islands across the lagoon appear misty and illusory as we run to catch the ferry to the island of

Burano. Our vaparetto passes Casino deli Spiriti on the corner, its windows looking blankly out at the lagoon. Behind us, the city seems harried by haze, sky shimmering above slowly vanishing bell towers. I inhale Adriatic air and a musky scent, more algae than seaweed. A gull above us flutters white, caught by the sun. We pass the vaparetto stop for San Michele, clustered conifers behind its brick walls, a glimpse of a domed chapel in the centre.

On the island of Murano (home to the glassmakers and ill-fated little Guiseppina Gabriel Carmelo) there stands a stone lighthouse, its light a beacon in the fog. As the islands come into sharper focus, it is now Venice that seems unreal – ill-defined and dreamlike. Lining the streets of island town Burano are cheerful rows of low, pastel-perfect houses. Legend tells that the homes in this fishing community were painted as a response to fog; the houses acted as colourful beacons across the lagoon, with rainbow facades ensuring they could be seen by fisherman as they travelled home with their catch, in frequent fog. Burano's streets are quiet – laundry strung on lines across the houses, lilac sheets matching walls in shades of heather, like a tonal paint chart. From the far end of the island we look out across the salt flats that stretch into the glass lagoon – small seagrass-covered islands with narrow, upright wooden posts dotted between. Here, sea touches sky, and this wetland landscape is reminiscent of the Flag Fen post alignment – that borderland between life and death with the ancestral Otherworld concealed in its depths. On the boat back, encircled by tranquil blue as the vaparetto follows the wooden waymarkers, I watch the shadowy city rise up on the horizon, poised between serene water and unblemished sky.

*

In Venice, death comes even to the water; the moments of peak high or low tide when the waters seem to pause, hanging briefly motionless before turning, are called by Venetians *morto d'acqua* (dead water). It is the alchemical blend of land and water that lends Venice its unmistakable magic, but water (and time) also represent threat. Like the potentially disappearing fog, this city is at risk from climate change, endangered by the very waters that make it so unique. In an introduction to *Venice and the Anthropocene: An Ecocritical Guide*, Lucio De Capitani explains: 'Phenomena that are said to characterise the Anthropocene, the era in which humans became geological agents on a planetary level – have become everyday issues of the lagoon environment.' These phenomena include extreme weather and extinctions. The interwoven fates of humans and their environment are urgent and perceptible here in a way that has so far often been overlooked elsewhere. If Venice can develop what Lucio De Capitani calls a 'new, sustainable, fairer vision of the future', it could offer a model for wider planetary solutions. The water city is, he says – like the planet – in need of a new story. In May 2019, British graffiti artist Banksy (whose work is a familiar sight to me from the walls of his hometown Bristol, where I studied and lived for many years) stencilled a mural entitled 'Migrant Child' on a building in Venice near Campiello Mosca – we happen upon it completely by chance, crossing a bridge. The image, sprayed onto the wall of a crumbling brick palazzo, depicts a child in a lifejacket standing down at the waterline, holding up a firing pink distress flare. The juxtaposition of street art and fading grandeur is deliberately destabilising, but far more unsettling is the salient meaning of the piece. Six months after the mural's creation, in November

2019, it was submerged by floods – the distressed child engulfed by rising waters became immediately emblematic of the desperate need for climate action.

On a wall near the Rialto fish market, an exhibition poster has been pasted. 'Everybody Talks About The Weather', it says. Under the arches, the scent of fish is strong and vendors call out their wares. Seagulls tiptoe across wet paving stones in among the feet of shoppers, hoping for scraps. I go to find the exhibition along a dead-end *calle* that leads to the Grand Canal, and I step into the serenity of the Fondazione Prada in hope of finding fog through art. The exhibition's premise is that talking about the weather can help us find a way to approach the intimidating but crucial challenge of the climate crisis. 'Far from the comforting inanity it has long been made out to be,' reads an explanatory board, 'talking about the weather today means talking about the future of both humankind and our only home, planet Earth.'

I find familiar artists reproduced among the exhibition's meteorological art: a cloudy Turner entitled *Rain, Steam and Speed – The Great Western Railway* depicting the air pollution of the Industrial Revolution, a painting that has been described as being about both progress and loss; a Monet, *Impression Sunrise*, in which, the exhibition guide suggests, we see 'the foggy omen of industrialisation'; and a Friedrich painting that captures a fearful aspect of the sublime, *The Sea of Ice*. Their collective presence feels less of a coincidence and more of a portent. I have observed weather that was once comparatively predictable altering day on day. I have been keeping a fog diary – recording every incidence of fog, every mention, every wisp. There is no doubt in my mind that even since last year fog has been far less frequent where I live. Had I not been taking note I might have failed to notice, but I am certain that our weather is changing fast, and yes, we do need to talk about it.

When I step, dazed, back out onto the streets, Venice wears the hazy winter sunshine like an expensive silk gown. It slides pearlescent over grand palazzos and anonymous backstreets alike, as light pools in puddles on the pavements. In Venice, this pure, end-of-the-day winter light is sensual – what Joseph Brodsky called 'a private light'. The light glimmers as it moves across the city's surfaces – shimmying down facades, tenderly touching windows and doorways, haloing passers-by with its glow. Water ripples – a fish flitting beneath – and the light glitters the surface of the canal like the diamonds that sparkle in Tiffany's window behind Piazza San Marco: light is dressing the city in the precious jewels of which she is so deserving. In the window of an expensive clothes shop a few doors down from the jewellers, sequin dresses drip like iridescent mermaid tails. Under the archways of the arcade beside the piazza, hundreds of silver baubles are jumbled, spread along a tarpaulin across the floor. The city is gathering her festive finery – a decoration-dotted tree already standing in the centre of the piazza, facing out to the lagoon and the sea beyond.

Last trip, on my birthday, Dan surprised me with a visit to the opera. On our way in the dark, we got lost and, hurrying through *calli*, I had no idea of our destination until we climbed the steps of the opera house, its foyer aglitter – sparkling chandeliers infinitely reflected in gold-rimmed, distressed-glass mirrors. It was the closest I have come to the sensation of stepping directly into a dream. Now, as night falls and I make my way back to the apartment, the streets of Castello twinkle with Christmas lights – a tunnelling cascade of icicles. Streetlights point their pools downwards, muted enough for the stars to remain clearly visible, as the light of the almost-full moon – the most private light of all – replaces that of the sun.

Here in the water city, every sense is stimulated: sight, hearing, touch, taste and smell, not to mention the sense of direction, for which labyrinthine streets prove a constant challenge. Venice is a city of sensory delight – a work of art, a poem made physical – but this excess of sublimity can be overwhelming. Tiziano Scarpa playfully writes in *Venice is a Fish* that 'too much splendour seriously damages your health', bemoaning the Venetians' forced daily exposure to endless visual wonders. This, he suggests, explains their devotion to Santa Lucia (the patron saint of sight). He posits that an annual visit to the blinded saint must heal 'beauty-clouded' eyes. How might eyes clouded by excess beauty experience a cloud of fog? I imagine fog draping the city in its folds: a dampening of colour, a flattening of light. I picture the skyline diminishing, cloud merging with water, churches, bridges and towers receding into grey. Perhaps, in this glory-filled city, a transfiguring curtain of fog could offer a necessary visual pause, a period of soothing respite, an escape from scintillation. But does fog hide beauty, or does it enhance it? Joseph Brodsky described the *nebbia* as 'thick, blinding, and immobile', so much so that to pass through it is to leave a tunnel behind you, and Jan Morris said of winter Venice that 'when you walk back across Dorsoduro, shafts of lights from opening doors punctuate the fog'. The dense fog is solid enough to hold its shape, so that the lamplight must slice it like a knife through star-sweet *pandoro*. Yet despite fog's concealing quality, even this happening – the intersect of light and fog – creates an image of beauty.

The next day, in the early morning, I notice canal-water shimmers reflected on the apartment ceiling. Venetians call this phenomenon *fa la vecia*, which Erica Jong translates to 'do as the old woman does' or, idiomatically, 'to squint'. We close the balcony doors and step into the day. Barges glide through quiet canals, heavy with supplies for the hotels and restaurants: wine and water, laundry, or milk. Delivery men unload on the quays, tossing boxes easily, one to another. We pass a floating fruit and vegetable stall replete with produce, the stallholder peeling fleshy globe artichokes, a growing pile of green petals beside him. Dad loves to watch the industry beneath Venice's beauty: the work boats that keep the city alive. He is fascinated by the mechanics of this place – the behind-the-scenes func-tionality that allows for the magic – and he has been frequently impressed by the skilled boatmanship of busy skippers.

We make our way to Piazza San Marco before the crowds accumulate, searching (rather macabrely) for an executioner's block on the corner of the towering white church, Basilica di San Marco Evangelista. Beneath a confection of carved marble we find it, a section of virtually unadorned column. This is the spot where a young Venetian named Pietro Faccioli is said to have been decapitated, having been unjustly accused of the murder of a nobleman. Above the block, at the top of the sea-facing facade, two lamps burn beside a mosaic image of the Virgin of the Sea. Just as Brent Tor church was built for Saint Michael following deliverance at sea, these lamps are said to have been donated by a sailor who survived a shipwreck, in gratitude to the Madonna to whom he prayed. The lights were said to be lit during executions to provide comfort to the condemned, and tradition tells that the flames now flicker in atonement by the Republic for the wrongful death of Pietro – who was known as the 'little baker-boy'. On foggy nights, when damp weather creeps into the piazza from the sea, is it said that scarlet spatters of blood appear on the column top – the poor innocent baker-boy's bloody revenge.

'There are some places in Venice', writes Lauren Elkin in *Flaneuse* (an exploration of women walking in cities), 'that, like Brigadoon, only emerge from the mist once in a hundred years.' She likens the city's twisting streets – which seem to 'rearrange themselves dextrously' – to a dealer shuffling cards. In an unspooling, shifting labyrinth, becoming disorientated is unavoidable, even desirable: a state which would only be heightened were Venice to become swathed in fog. '*Getting lost* is the only place worth going to,' suggests Tiziano Scarpa, and so I deliberately do. Dad and I go our separate ways to explore, and I aimlessly stroll, ignoring the map in my bag and the satnav on my phone, trusting to whim and following nothing but intuition around the curves of corners. Virginia Woolf, in 'Street Haunting', wrote that walking was a way to 'shed the self', and Rebecca Solnit suggests that for Woolf, 'getting lost was not a matter of geography so much as identity, a passionate desire, even an urgent need, to become no one and anyone'. I recognise this desire from my walks in the fog, and here too, in the endless, unreliable back streets, I feel the jostle and shift of my own past and present selves and – somewhere deeper – the insistent whisper of my fog-self. I understand the urge to shimmy free of the heavy weight of a daily self, and I yearn for the metamorphosis that fog can bring.

A savoury scent wafts past – someone's lunch is cooking. I hear splashes echo between the buildings, the clatter of trolley wheels on cobblestones, a jingle of keys. In an endless, echoing dialogue between city and water-time, buildings sway on the canal surface, and light reflected up from the water quivers over the faces of the buildings. At noon, the bells start to ring and a painted sign on the wall lets me know I have entered *sestiere* San Polo. It is the first time I've been to this area of the city and so I sit for a while in the sunshine, in front of a covered well at the centre of a campo. A little lemon tree, bearing fruit, is dappling brick walls with shadow. Beside me, a wide set of water steps lead down into the canal and the tuned wheezing of an accordion approaches, growing gradually louder – a gondola is on its way. A white feather dances across stone and the shadow of my skirt shifts in the breeze as a group of young schoolchildren pass close by, laughing. Surrendering to these streets is a kind of sweetness – if I sit in this unknown campo for long enough, perhaps all the sensory delights of Venice will come to me.

In the labyrinth there is a constant interplay between noise and silence. Sometimes, all that can be heard is the gentle lapping of the water, but there are other sounds that echo, and they often have a ghostly quality: bells, voices, footsteps. In Daphne du Maurier's short story 'Don't Look Now' (later adapted into an uncanny, fog-dampened film by Nicolas Roeg), the protagonist follows echoing footsteps through a maze of Venetian streets, drawn by the sobbing sound of what he takes to be a crying child in a pixie hood. The consequences are chilling and horrific, and the silence that follows is endless. Venetian fog brings particular sounds of its own. Jan Morris wrote that on 'foggy winter nights, when the city is blanketed in gloom and damp, you can hear the far-away tinkling of the bell-buoys out in the lagoon'. Bells from the sea provide a delicate echo to the church bells of the city. Another fog-formed sound that floats in across the water is the boom of foghorns from distant ships. When it fills up the city and darkens the streets, making them its own, fog brings a stilled quality of sound that is softer than silence. If you focus carefully, and learn to pay attention, Tiziano Scarpa says, 'you can listen to the fog'.

But the fog the forecast promised me has been slipping away, and so on our last day in Venice I go out early in search of it. Between the towers of the Arsenale, an enormous yellow shooting star has blossomed – picked out in Christmas lights. As I cross the bridge and walk towards the riva to meet the lagoon, a street-sweeper greets a cafe-owner putting out chairs with a cheerful 'Ciao!' I pass the giant anchor outside the naval history museum and stop by the quayside to look out at the island of Giudecca opposite (where Dan and I once had lunch in a hidden garden) – it has had all the colour bleached from it. The 'ancient lagoonal mists' are edging, as is their tendency, across the water and towards the city. Islands in the far distance are cloaked in low fog, and boats pass with their lights on. Giudecca's church bells chime seven o'clock, and a deep bell behind me rings sonorously in answer. Beside the water, an ornate, triple-headed lilac glass streetlamp flickers out on the final chime. The air is cold and I watch my breath mingle with emergent fog. I begin walking along the riva, passing dog-walkers, runners, solitary strollers and pigeons.

Four photographers with tripods are waiting for sunrise and, beyond them, across in Dorsuduro, the smooth white dome of Santa Maria della Salute merges into the sky.

Turner, who visited Venice on more than one occasion, portrayed a strikingly similar scene in an 1840 watercolour from his *Grand Canal and Giudecca Sketchbook*. Called *Sunset over Santa Maria della Salute and the Dogana*, it is described by Evan R. Firestone as 'among his most vaporous watercolours'. In it, the sky and Grand Canal are a mirrored wash of pale, hazy grey, the church an imprecise, shadowy presence reflected in the water. Turner used a painting technique called white ground: a white base over which he added detail and colour. 'The luminosity of the Venetian paintings,' Firestone writes, 'is attributable to the white ground.' Finding misty sublimity in art can be, like stepping into the labyrinth, another way in which to lose ourselves and become, in some small way, transformed.

I cross Piazza San Marco, where wooden walkways have appeared overnight in preparation for *acqua alta*; water bubbles up through the storm sewers. There are just a few days now until November's full moon, which is called the frost moon or sometimes ... the fog moon. It is almost high tide, and as I walk purposelessly alongside the canals, water climbs the walls, creeping up over the line of barnacles that marks its usual level. On the lagoon around the city, mist rises from the sea like steam, but it has yet to infiltrate the streets, although the morning air is chill, clammy and unfocused. The colours of the buildings are dimmed and the water has lost its clarity – this morning, there are no reflections. A discarded silver balloon floats under a bridge, and a florist arranges bouquets behind fogged-up windows. In front of Teatro La Fenice – the opera house – I pass a pair of police officers slowly walking the streets. I wonder who, besides me, might hope now for fog; who would prefer a cold, damp city to a sunny, clear one? Photographers, and perhaps artists, but also people who thrive in the dark: people with something to hide. In the event of fog, Joseph Brodsky counselled taking your cue from the city and sharing in its invisibility. This is a seductive suggestion – my fog-self is drawn to disappearance – but passing an open door, I catch coffee on the breeze, and I am reminded that I have not yet had my breakfast.

As I walk back along the riva, the air seems thick enough that I could catch a handful of it, the sun so swaddled by layers of cloud it looks more like the moon. Then, out towards the mainland, it breaks through – I see a patch of coruscating orange where it reaches down to the water. At my feet, waves splash insistently against the edge of water steps, and gondolas bob, moored in a line to wooden posts. The emerging day has that quality of golden, caressing, secret light that comes only when sun and mist meet: not with the clear definition of sunbeams, but in a blended, mellow cocktail of water and light. This time of day is what photographers call magic hour – the period just after sunrise (or before sunset), when light is at its most flattering and flawless. I stand in a perfect city, blessed by perfect light, and although I am missing Dan and our boys – feeling ready to leave tomorrow – a part of me wants to disappear: taking up mist's invisible mantle and slipping away to find myself a room in a quiet palazzo with a desk by the window and a view of the canal. I picture this shade of a self who has never been, and wish for another lifetime in which to stay and write: to watch the dawn, wait for the mist, and tell stories that now I'll never know. I briefly envisage how it might feel to melt into these streets and become someone else entirely, as if cleansed and remade by the waters of the Adriatic, but I know I cannot – I must return to my promises.

I buy a couple of buttery *cornetti* in a paper bag and take them back to share with Dad on the balcony. That afternoon we walk to the Scuola Grande di San Rocco (sometimes called 'Venice's Sistine Chapel') to see Tintoretto's fresco cycle in the Chapter Hall. Surrounded on all sides by glossy marble and incredible art, we view the ceiling paintings as reflections, using hand-held mirrors. Eventually, starry-eyed from splendour, we step out into the streets. At first, I wonder if gazing at the gold ceiling has affected my vision – the air looks milky and I can't see clearly, but it's not the Tintorettos: it's fog, swirling into the city from the lagoon, streaking through the streets like smoke. It's patchy and it's out on the margins – almost at the point where the city ceases to be – but this is fog and it is in Venice, and I have found it.

We take a vaparetto along the Grand Canal; peering down side canals as we pass, I see fog at the ends and edges of the city, making its way in from the sea on every side. It is now twilight, the time that E. M. Forster (writing of a different Italian city) called 'the hour of unreality – the hour, that is, when unfamiliar things are real'. Venice feels more dreamlike than ever, its beauty enhanced in the half-light. Fog alters the city, just as the city alters those who surrender to it. I take it all in. Like the mist at the stone circles on the Beara Peninsula, this fog has melded with the sunshine, its gleam and softness a cumulative magic of mist and light. In the bewitching dusky light, the facades of the palazzos that line the Grand Canal gleam pastel-pale, and the people flowing over bridges are but shadows. Clouds are tinted pink and edged with gold – as if they have been painted by Tintoretto himself.

Later, as I take one last look from the window of the train, I am ready to depart, but my conversation with Venice is not over – I know this city of wonder will call me back, although who I will be in that future moment, I cannot yet tell. I leave with words scribbled in notebooks, photographs locked in my camera, a bag of *cantuccini* to eat in my seat and three carefully wrapped Murano glass Christmas trees for my children. My fog-self has seized a souvenir of her own: the fog that arrived by stealth and shiver has seeped into my bones and she gathers it greedily up. I, like the city, have been transfigured by the fog. As towns and rivers fly by outside, I begin to wonder if it might in fact be following me home: passing from Italy into Switzerland, the peaks of the snow-topped mountains disappear into mist. The train sways along a lake where Dad used to holiday as a child, sun sinking into glacial turquoise water. Snow slips down larch-thick mountain slopes, and then, at the top of the Matterhorn, a cloud-puff drift of fog; powder snow mixed with mist, the summit disappeared from view.

The next morning, through the lowlands of northern France, mist drifts over frosty fields, and I see a flash of rainbow above hazy hills, despite not a hint of rain. In the end, I find fog where I started: up on the escarpment above my house, where it hangs densely. Driving home from the station, the air is opaque and I feel as if I'm moving through a solid entity, following the cats' eyes down the centre of the road like a white breadcrumb trail through the darkness.

*

A few days after the night of the full fog moon, I wake to find the town coated in a chalk-white cloud of fog, blanketed by a hoar frost that has captured everything in its path: it is December. In a hurry, I gather warm layers and I rush to the woods. The air temperature is several degrees below zero and freezing air stings my skin. This winter fog is different to the fog of autumn; its droplets – icy against my cheek – have the texture of snow. In the lane I pass a robin in the hedgerow, fluffing itself up against the cold – around it, frosted umbellifer heads twinkle like snowflake stars. Draping over bushes, twists of Clematis vitalba stretch like snow spiders. The green nettles have been rendered stingless by the cold, the veins on the back of their leaves stiff, their edges frosted.

On the ground along the edge of the woods, moss makes a carpet of tiny snow-sprinkled fir trees, while the full-sized, frost-dusted treetops emerge from a sunken cloud of fog and reach up to the sky. The highest branches of the trees are illuminated startling white by the sun. A little way above them, at the bottom of the sky, the ghost of the waning moon is visible. This fading fog-frost moon has used the last vestiges of its strength to make me an immaculate morning. Gathering heat, the sun sends clearly defined rays down into the fog, darting through the trees. There's a dialogue taking place here in the woods between sun – its warmth blessing the frozen leaves – fog and moon, so faint and cold. I cannot know the celestial secrets they share, but my fog-self thrills at the sight. I nod my gratitude to the fog moon, and I stride on.

Dan has come up to meet me, and together we take the path that leads to the top of the hill – from which we can usually see out across the Severn Vale as far as Wales – today it has disappeared into white: the grass, the brambles, the bushes and the trees. The sun has vanished from view and fog is everywhere, thicker and colder than ever. A bench on the edge of the hill – usually a viewing point for sunsets across the valley – looks out only onto dense, featureless white: fog and frost have merged. Of all the foggy mornings, these are my favourite kind – the immersion, the quiet, the sense of a world made new. In weather like this, my fog-self murmurs that anything is possible, and on this glimmer-bright day, I believe her. Dan and I return through the woods, skeletal white ghost leaves rustling, frozen beneath our feet. Along the path, puddles – cracked with ice – shine like glass. Deep between the trees, the frost is thicker; each twig and individual ivy leaf, each string of creeper and frond of grass edged in glitter. My fingers and toes are numb now, but I ignore the pain and wander further into this temporary icy realm. The crown of the sky has returned and the treetops stretch towards it as the woods remain hidden by fog. Around the woodland edges, radiant sunlight blends with fog – the same golden light I saw at magic hour in Venice. We stop together, entranced.

Eventually, the need for warmth wins out and we turn for home. On the hillside, smoke from cottage chimneys drifts up, mingling with the fog. The town below has vanished, shrouded and silent. There in the valley, the gold clock on the church tower chimes solemnly, its face dulled. Gravestones loom from the shadows, dusted with frost, and in the centre of the churchyard is a tree covered in clusters of mistletoe – its pearl-white berries gleaming – which will surely be raided come midwinter. The high street is turbid with fog and a man balances up a ladder, mounting a Christmas tree onto the front of a shop. Minuscule webs cluster at the tops of telephone poles like frosted tinsel. At home, I listen to the jackdaws converse in the beech tree opposite before they take to the air and fly over the rooftops. I defrost my hands on the radiator, wondering if the fog will fade before nightfall. When my middle son returns from mountain biking in the frozen quarry, I ask him if it was foggy. 'So foggy,' he says, 'that the spiderwebs were glowing!' I smile at his way of seeing and we all sit down for soup, the street covered by an icy, white quilt.

I have crossed rivers, seas and countries in search of fog. I encountered clouds of niwl, a covering of haag, rising ceo and twists of calìgo, but the enchanted fog that transmutes the world into a dream found me here, pressing with icy insistence up against my little window. In over a year of intentional chasing – venturing far beyond the familiar fog that slips into my everyday – it has become apparent that even when I didn't see or directly experience it, fog was there in the flora and the texture of the locations I visited. It was woven into the words, events and stories that belong to them. We see fog as something that floats over the surface – drifting by and passing through – but its tendrils are tightly plaited through the layered landscape. When fog inhabits a place, it leaves behind an indefinable trace – a feather-light memory of cloud's quietly reverberating touch. Subtly, silently, fog makes the world anew; it alters all that it envelops, which is why I cannot help but seek it. Beyond all else, it is fog's transformative magic that I crave.

Epilogue

I wake at dawn, in that charged pause between night and day. Deep midnight-blue sky is fading to pale and the last of the stars are flickering out. The waning moon, reflected in the water of the canal, is so perfect a crescent I could dip my hand into the water and scoop it up: a clean slice of lemon, a sliver of fingernail. Along the bank, a row of skeletal January trees turn their elegant branches in front of the canal's mirror. From either side of the water a robin and a song thrush carol loudly to one another. It is the morning of the Twelfth Night – the penultimate of the Celtic Omen Days – and during this meaningful period of in-between time, which is said to hint at what the months to come might offer, I have been looking for signs.

In the night, as the moon shone, rippling waterlight was reflected onto the wooden ceiling of the narrowboat where I slept – *fa la vecia*, glimpsed as I surfaced from a dream. But I float far from Venice; these are the constant waters of the Gloucester and Sharpness Canal, running parallel with the River Severn. Just a few miles away from where I sleep on this, my parents' boat, the wrecks of *Arkendale H* and *Wastdale H* are being consumed once more by the tide, and released again. All week the weather forecast has promised fog, and day after day it has disappeared from the map. I am bitterly disappointed – I had hoped to wake here fully submerged in the Severn fog, which, like the fog in Alice Oswald's poem, often follows the bottom of the valley so closely that when seen from above on the peak, it seems to form a second, somnolent river of cloud, lying alongside the Severn. But perhaps fog's absence is in itself an omen.

By paying close attention to fog – the ground cloud I fear to be fading – I have tried (imperfectly, truthfully) to bear witness, looking for beauty in a darkening world, for abundance where there so often is none, for clarity through a misted lens. I have chased fog but so often I have found only glimpses of it: a drift of cloud, a shiver of mist, a quickening on the periphery of my vision. Moments of submersion in the full depths of fog have been few, for all I have sought them out, and this has heightened their intensity. Each time I have found myself thinking: *what if this is my last foggy morning?* What I did not expect to discover, hidden in the rising wreaths, was a fog-self: a way of merging with the world, of letting the world in. Somewhere across the years the little girl who ran so freely along the edge of the moor, wind catching at her hair, lost a sense of herself – perhaps through grief, or work, or motherhood. In the fog, I found what was missing. Fog itself is a combination of elements: a suspension of water in air. It is a threshold, a state change, a sensation; it is the strangeness in the ordinary.

Fog absorbs me, even as I (through my skin and hair) absorb it. It cocoons me, the external world receding and my internal world becoming more vivid. In the fog, I look within: I never feel more truly myself than when I am surrounded by fog. It shows me not just who I am, but who I need to become. When it falls, suddenly nothing looks the same. In that moment, it seems that fog – the feeling of it, its physical reality, its metaphorical meanings – is all there ever will be. Anything beyond the fog becomes nothing but a memory, until the scene shuffles and the sky reappears. Even when the cloud has passed, my fog-self lingers on, wide-eyed and sky-startled. Interludes of fog are brief and passing but now that she has unfurled from within, that once-buried part of me – my fog-self – remains. She, to whom the heavens are wondrously strange, perceives the world with a freshness and clarity that had been lost to me. Tuning in to her murmurs, I become acutely aware of colours and patterns that others might miss. My fog-self is the part of me that feels the world fully and deeply; she offers not just a way of seeing, but a way of being. I hold fast to her, for it is she who shows me precious glimmers in the darkness.

Perhaps, though, she is not as invisible as I thought; it seems that the people who love me have begun to perceive her too. In the folder on my phone entitled 'fog diary', I keep notes on every instance of fog I experience and I also collect together the lines and photographs I receive on foggy days – even when the fog is hundreds of miles away – and there are many. 'I'm on the train,' Dan texts me. 'Lots of fog across Wiltshire and we're running slow.' Earlier in the week, as I stirred the porridge, he had sent me simply the word 'FOG'. To me, these are expressions of love. 'Driving through Dartmoor in the mist,' comes an Instagram message from my niece, 'very atmospheric'. My eldest teenager sends me photographs of the foggy valley from the bus: '*J'ai pensé que tu aimerais*,' he writes. On days when it is foggy in our town, my boys almost always text me from the school run with 'it's foggy out here, Mum', or 'there's fog'. My friends know that if we are in the cafe when fog falls I am liable to jump up, coffee half-drunk, and go in search of it. Passing me after school drop-off, as fog begins to curl around the town, they never need to ask why I am hurrying away. Sometimes, early in the morning, a friend will send me a note reading only: 'fog alert!' I see the words 'fog alert', but I hear: 'I thought of you'. I hear: 'I see the world in the way that you do'. These communications tell me someone is thinking of me. They tell me there is wonder out there and I'm not alone in choosing to see it.

Last summer, we visited my brother Tom in Vermont, during which time we stayed for a few days in a shiplap pond house with him, his wife Jean, and their Sheepadoodle, Arf Garfunkel. Behind the house, where the garden stretched down to the water (to me, a large swimming lake, but in Vermont, a pond), a narrow wooden bridge crossed lily-padded shallows to a tiny island, a figure-of-eight spit with twin pine trees and a wooden bench for sundowners. One night, after a day of swimming and sunshine, I was almost asleep when Tom's fluffy dog padded up the stairs and nosed open the door to my room; in the deep rural darkness, fog had fallen over the lake. My brother, watching late-night cricket with Dan, had seen the fog and mentioned my name. On hearing this, Garf, sweetest of dogs, had slipped out the door and up to my bedroom to find me. I followed him down the stairs – one hand tangled in his fur, the other rubbing my eyes – and Tom opened the back door.

In the garden, the air was humming with insects. Fog had arrived from nowhere, heavy and fast – the sky was thick velvet, and the stars had disappeared. In the shallows, a fish splashed. The two of us crouched over the damp grass and watched the air shiver and thicken as the dog, delighted, ran across the bridge onto the island, barely visible against the backdrop of the fogged lake. My brother laughed; the dog, he told me, was proud. I felt so close to him then, in that misty moment in the strange garden (a place far from where our home once was, and mine still is). I was sleepy, the mosquitos were gathering around me in my pyjamas, and the next day I would be leaving, but I knew as I listened to his dear voice in the dark that I would always remember us sharing the lake's midnight magic.

I once attended a writing workshop in which the teacher said of her work that obsession was stronger than fear, and although the details are lost to me, those words remained. When I'm chasing fog, my obsession is stronger than my fear. Throughout this fog-chasing journey, I have put myself into situations I wouldn't otherwise seek out: I have slept alone in places that shook me (the heart of a moor, the side of a lonely canal); I have climbed a mountain and swum at the top, walked through empty marshes and ventured time after time deep into foggy woods with only my camera for company. Alone amid the trees, fog flows around me like energetic inspiration – creative flow made visible. I follow an unknown path, meandering without purpose as cool air touches my face in greeting. Fog is made up of water droplets but to me it is also made up of words, thousands of them – clouding the air and tickling my cheeks – fog always has a message to share.

On foggy days, I attempt to catch the weather's meaning, with fractured voice recordings on my phone and photographs to remind me of the tones in the trees, and of how the woods were transmuted when the light broke briefly through in scattered rays. If I am alone in the woods and a figure looms out unexpectedly through the fog, I experience a rush of adrenaline: suddenly startled, always wary. But I am my obsession, and the thrill is also stronger than the fear. A walk in the fog gives me a feeling of intense connection to the weather, to the light, to the trees and to the ground on which I stand: it is the truest way I have found of becoming enmeshed with the world – and, often, with others too.

As I have chased fog, through a year and out the other side, fog has become increasingly difficult to find. I have learned, thanks to a fog photographer I connected with on Instagram, to use the Ventusky app, with which I can switch between satellites, using data from the skies to watch fog's passage across a map. This seems to me a kind of inexplicable sorcery. But even using the secrets of the satellites, fog is not easily predicted – the days that promise fog are few, and the days that bring it are far fewer. In the January lockdown of 2021, I recall day after stunning day of hoar frost and freezing fog. We walked for hours in the fog-fuzzed valley, flasks of hot chocolate in our backpacks, as my children lifted disks of pearlescent ice in their gloved hands, laughter clouding out to meet the fog. This January so far there has been almost ceaseless rain and storms bringing terrible flooding, including in the Severn Valley. The weather is changing, but although we can track it with data and satellites, weather is not something that exists on the other side of a screen – it is here, it is now, it is us. The seasons are slipping, and the weather patterns we remember no longer exist. We must recognise the pace of change that we face, and find ways to live that protect the dancing skies and this dear, only earth.

Collectively, we tend to take fog's existence for granted, ignoring, or only occasionally – if it interferes with our plans – resenting it. We sleepwalk on, unaware of its potential disappearance, which is characteristic of how we respond to much of the non-human world; so many species are edging into extinction and more are fading from knowledge, memory and common parlance. In *The Lost Words*, Robert Macfarlane and Jackie Morris, who seek to redress this dimming, write of 'the old, strong magic of being spoken aloud'. This word-summoning magic can bring back the lost by using song and story to remind us of the natural world we have taken for granted, speaking it back into being. Fog is a quiet weather in comparison to fierce sun or heavy storms, but this does not mean we should remain quiet about it. Compared to the new climate change-fuelled, increasingly violent and unpredictable weather systems, fog also seems steady. But fog does not always feel benign – it can unexpectedly immerse us, spin us around and confuse us; it can unsettle and frighten us. Its decreased visibility and tendency to absorb pollution has always meant that fog can be powerful, dangerous even, but it does not often demand our attention and it is, albeit gently, diminishing. With our rapidly changing climate we risk losing so much, including the swirling wonder of fog. I do so believe that we need to talk about the weather: we need to sing and write poems about the weather; we need to cry and scream about the weather, to tell its tales.

One foggy day, when my three boys were small, we filled a large jam jar with battery-powered fairy lights and carried it up to the woods. The boys held the jar, and I took their photographs, the straight, striped trunks behind them like perfect arboreal wallpaper. They giggled, delighted by the juxtaposition of glitter and gloom, passing the lights between them like a secret. Afterwards, bored of having their pictures taken, they slung arms across one another's shoulders, and, leaving the jar behind, walked into the silent, foggy woods, deep in conversation, caught up in a game and utterly unafraid. Perhaps somewhere between the trees they found fog-selves of their own. Immersed in an imaginary world of their creation, they already knew what I had yet to discover: that there are always, always stories hidden in the fog – stories that reveal deeper meanings. The future, like the fog, is opaque, but into it we can carry these stories like beacons of light. If we listen, fog has much to teach us: about the landscape, the weatherscape and about who we are. We are all made of water – it passes through us and moves on, into the rain, into the river, into the ocean, into the fog. Each of us is fluid, mutable, magic, and we are not distinct from nature, we *are* nature. We are fog.

On the boat, awake now, my fog-self shows me dust motes floating in the sunshine and the *fa la vecia* has returned. I think of the months I have spent dreaming of, pining for, obsessing over and chasing fog. I remember a morning earlier this winter, the frosty grass powdery and ice-sparkled. From my loft-room window I could see streaks of white fog floating above the valley, but when I walked down into the valley itself I found it to be the kind of fog that is always slightly out of reach: just a little way further down the path, or a few steps on from where I stood. The air was unclear, as if sleepy dust had yet to be rubbed from my eyes. It was a fog that left me wanting more; it seemed to hide around every corner: a whisper, a hint, a softening, a smoothing. For an instant it seemed as if I might have breathed it into being – clouds into cold air – or perhaps had only dreamt it. Sometimes, when I explain what I am writing about, people say, 'You're writing a book about fog?' – understandably perplexed. Perhaps fog is a strange thing to obsess over. But aren't we all chasing something, all of the time? We can chase money, success or happiness … but in the end, isn't it all just as ephemeral as fog? I won't stop chasing once the final page is turned, not as long as there are foggy mornings. It's easy to get lost in the fog, but fog is also somewhere that imperceptible things can be found, including parts of ourselves – the disappearing mist-wraiths whisper us a message, if only we will listen.

I have written a love letter to fog. I do not wish for it to become an elegy.

Notes

Introduction

page 4   '50 per cent drop in "low-visibility" events': www.researchgate.
net/publication/248828332_Decline_of_fog_mist_and_haze_
in_Europe_over_the_past_30years

page 4   'disastrous consequences for ecology': https://insideclimatenews.
org/news/10102021/coastal-fog-global-warming

1: With Vision Obscured – River Severn

page 8   'When air becomes cooled': www.metoffice.gov.uk/
weather/learn-about/weather/types-of-weather/fog/
how-do-you-forecast-fog

page 8   'thick cloud close to the land or sea': https://dictionary.
cambridge.org/dictionary/english/fog

page 8   'under one thousand metres, it's fog': www.metoffice.gov.
uk/weather/learn-about/weather/types-of-weather/fog/
difference-mist-and-fog

page 9   'long-strawed, weak, scattered grass': C.T. Onions (Ed.), *The
Oxford Dictionary of English Etymology* (Oxford: Clarendon Press,
1966), p. 366.

page 9   'Old Norse *fjuk*': https://www.etymonline.com/word/fog

page 9   'uncanny nature having ancient roots': https://www.etymonline.
com/search?q=mist

page 9   'linger in high-elevation areas': Gavin Pretor-Pinney, *The
Cloudspotter's Guide* (London: Hodder Headline, 2006), pp. 83–4.

page 9   'like a lid on a jar of cloud': www.metoffice.gov.uk/weather/
learn-about/weather/types-of-weather/temperature/
temperature-inversion

page 11   'leads us "to the threshold of the unknown"': Evan R.
Firestone, *Mist and Fog in British and European Painting: Fuseli,
Friedrich, Turner, Monet and their Contemporaries* (London: Lund
Humphries, 2023), p. 68.

page 11   'appears larger, more sublime': quoted by Firestone, p. 70.

page 11   'an artistic effect productive of the strongest emotion':
www.tate.org.uk/art/art-terms/s/sublime

page 11   '*Rückenfigur*': Firestone, p. 70.

page 12   'lone enraptured male': www.lrb.co.uk/the-paper/v30/n05/
kathleen-jamie/a-lone-enraptured-male

page 12   'the reciprocal nature of vision': John Berger, *Ways of Seeing*
(London: Penguin, 1972), p. 9.

page 12   'not "dwarfed" by the landscape he surveys': Peter Moore, *The
Weather Experiment* (London: Chatto & Windus, 2015), p. 86.

page 13   'impossible to see the bow from inside the wheelhouse':
Chris Witts, *Severn Bridge Disaster* (Gloucester: River Severn
Publications, 2010), p. 13.

page 13   'vanished back into the fog': Ibid.

page 14   'fire was so intense that the sky was lit through the fog':
www.friendsofpurton.org.uk/severnb (testimony of Mr D.
White, Sharpness)

page 14   'fog-shrouded river': www.friendsofpurton.org.uk/severnb
(p. 17 of exhibition slides)

page 14   'prevent them from drifting any further': www.severntales.
co.uk/severn-bridge-disaster.html

page 15   'erosive power of the Severn': https://en.wikipedia.org/wiki/
Purton_Hulks (accessed 30/10/23)

page 15   'Severn Bridge Disaster': www.friendsofpurton.org.uk/purton

page 17   'his wife Gwendolen in an underground cave': Geoffrey of
Monmouth, translated by Lewis Thorpe, *The History of The
Kings of Britain* (London: The Folio Society, 1966), p. 57.

page 17   'made Estrildis his queen': Ibid. p. 58.

page 17   'in Welsh, Afon Hafren; in English, River Severn': Thorpe,
pp. 57–8.

page 18   'The water-nymphs': www.gutenberg.org/files/19819/19819-
h/19819-h.htm lines 833–4.

page 18 'to aid a virgin, such as was herself': www.gutenberg.org/ files/19819/19819-h/19819-h.htm lines 852–6.

page 18 'visits the herds along the twilight meadows': www.gutenberg. org/files/19819/19819-h/19819-h.htm line 844.

page 18 'when her veil of mist is lifted by the sun': https://exemplore. com/legends/Sabrina-Fair-Goddess-of-the-Severn

page 19 'a fogbow is usually white in appearance': www.metoffice.gov. uk/weather/learn-about/weather/optical-effects/rainbows/ fogbow

page 19 'nature evokes the sublime': Firestone, p. 94.

page 19 'all the way across to Portishead': www. bristol247.com/news-and-features/news/ photographer-captures-rare-weather-phenomenon

page 19 'we are exposed to what he called its "aura"': Walter Benjamin, *The Work of Art in the Age of Mechanical Reproduction* translated by Harry Zohn from the 1935 essay in *Illuminations*, ed. Hannah Arendt (New York: Schocken Books, 1969), p. 4 https://web. mit.edu/allanmc/www/benjamin.pdf

page 20 'distance in time between the painting of the picture and one's own act of looking at it': Berger, p. 31.

page 20 'reflected in his choice of subject': Berger, p. 10.

page 21 'Lower Stone Beacon to Berkeley Pill': Newspaper article shared by https://twitter.com/MuseumThornbury

page 22 'replaced the elegant metal 1906 lighthouse tower in 2010': www.ibiblio.org/lighthouse/engw.htm

page 23 'barges "linked like strings of sausages"': newspaper article shared by https://twitter.com/MuseumThornbury

page 23 'the keeper of the lights': https://richedwardsart.com

page 25 'picked her posies of wild orchids': newspaper article shared by https://twitter.com/MuseumThornbury

page 26 '"lie with him" nearby': https:// insearchofholywellsandhealingsprings.com/the-source-new- series-contents/st-arilda-of-oldbury-on-severn-gloucestershire/#5

2: My Fog-Self – Dartmoor

page 32 'Powdermills, near Princetown': www.dartcom.co.uk/webcam

page 36 'Ministry of Defence training area': www.wildthingspublishing. com/wp-content/uploads/2016/04/WSWDD-8.pdf

page 38 'a gaunt and towering witch called Vixiana': the Dartmoor Folklore Map: https://www.plymouthherald.co.uk/news/history/legend-vixiana-sadistic-dartmoor-witch-4642118

page 38 'regarded by the pixies as theirs': William Crossing, *Folklore and Legends of Dartmoor* (Newton Abbot: Forest Publishing, 1997), p. 74.

page 39 'the true Dartmoor pixie has long since vanished into the mists': Ruth E. St Leger-Gordon, *The Witchcraft and Folklore of Dartmoor* (Newton Abbott: Peninsula Press, 2001), p. 17.

page 39 'Dartmoor spun me round': www.countryfile.com/podcast/legends-stories-tomcox

page 39 'Devon dialect word "wisht"': Guy Shrubsole, *The Lost Rainforests of Britain* (London: William Collins, 2022), p. 24.

page 39 'the Devil himself': www.legendarydartmoor.co.uk/2016/03/31/wistman

page 39 'extensive temperate rainforest': Shrubsole, p. 34.

page 40 'walking as seance': Robert Macfarlane, *The Old Ways: A Journey on Foot* (London: Penguin, 2013), p. 21.

page 40 'mingled with the procession': quoted by: Ruth St Leger-Gordon, *The Witchcraft and Folklore of Dartmoor* (Newton Abbott: Peninsula Press, 2001), p. 30.

page 41 'its name connotes "wise man"': www.legendarydartmoor.co.uk/2016/03/31/wistman/

page 43 'left to finish his church in peace': www.dartmoor.gov.uk/learning/dartmoor-legends/the-legend-of-brentor-church

page 45 'drawn into, and entranced by, the fog': https://www.theguardian.com/lifeandstyle/2019/dec/19/alice-oswald-exclusive-poem-mist

page 45 'soul gets caught in it': https://www.theguardian.com/lifeandstyle/2019/dec/19/alice-oswald-exclusive-poem-mist

page 45 'a convict has escaped from nearby Princetown': Arthur Conan Doyle, *The Hound of the Baskervilles* (Berkshire: Baker Street Press, 1902), p. 80.

page 46 'leave your own age behind you': Doyle, pp. 107–8.

page 46 'enormous coal-black hound': Doyle, p. 213.

page 46 'the one thing upon earth which could have disarranged my plans': Doyle, p. 210.

page 46 'the fog-wreaths came crawling round both corners of the house': Doyle, p. 211.

NOTES

page 47 '"white wool"-wrapped house': Doyle, p. 218.

page 48 'sunlight interacting with the water droplets': https://www.
metoffice.gov.uk/weather/learn-about/weather/optical-effects/
brocken-spectre

page 49 'so memorably aestheticised': Heather Clark, *Red Comet: The
Short Life and Blazing Art of Sylvia Plath* (London: Vintage, 2020),
p. 862.

page 50 'felt no strangeness in sun and wind and rain': Alfred Watkins,
The Old Straight Track (Reading: Abacus, 1970), p. xix.

page 51 'elemental or malignant spirit': St Leger-Gordon, p. 40.

page 52 'safe passage in the dusk': Macfarlane, p. 15.

3: Lost in the Fog – Meirionnydd, Wales

page 58 'healing and alchemical properties': www.plantlife.org.uk/uk/
nature-reserves-important-plant-areas/important-plant-areas/
cambrian-mountains-orefield

page 59 'part of me is always there': Susan Cooper, *Dreams and
Wishes: Essays on Writing for Children* (New York: Margaret K.
McElderry, 1996), p. 81.

page 59 'weather and skies and spells': Cooper, p. 94.

page 60 'the Brenin Llwyd I did not invent': Susan Cooper, *The Grey
King* (Middlesex: Puffin Books, 1975), p. 7.

page 60 'caught in his clutches!': Marie Trevelyan, *Folk-lore and Folk-
stories of Wales* (London: E Stock, 1909), p. 69.

page 60 'direct the mist's journey through the air': Rev. Elias Owen,
*Welsh Folk-lore: A Collection of the Folk Tales and Legends of
North Wales* (Oswestry and Wrexham: Woodall, Minshall
and Co., 1887), p. 142. https://www.gutenberg.org/
files/20096/20096-h/20096-h.htm

page 61 'welcomed into his "court of mists"': Trevelyan, p. 69.

page 61 'equivalent characters': https://research.bangor.ac.uk/portal/
files/40328713/2021_R_diger_AH_PhD.pdf p.116

page 62 'Cadair Idris is a place where people do get lost in the fog':
www.mountain.rescue.org.uk/news

page 63 'It becomes a little like a detective game, really': https://discover.
library.wales/discovery/fulldisplay?context=L&vid=44WHELF_
NLW:44WHELF_NLW_NUI&d ocid=alma99362383002419

page 63 'the thousand things that make the wild a text': Rebecca Solnit,

A Field Guide to Getting Lost (Edinburgh: Canongate, 2006), p. 10.

page 64 'even as the world turns to white': Nan Shepherd, *The Living Mountain* (London: Canongate, 2011), p. 44.

page 65 'so huge he used this mountain as a chair': https://coflein.gov.uk/en/site/406409

page 65 'studying the stars': http://www.earlybritishkingdoms.com/bios/idrisgmd.html

page 66 'he named that mountain as Cadair Idris': *The Tommy Tiernan Show* season 5. Episode 5, 11 May 2023.

page 66 'I entered the mystic': https://drmartinshaw.com/interview/

page 66 'sacred importance in the Iron Age': https://coflein.gov.uk/en/site/419531/ and https://coflein.gov.uk/en/site/402426

page 67 'under greater threat than even tropical rainforests': https://snowdonia.gov.wales/protect/conservation-work/celtic-rainforests-wales

page 67 'lichens make a fog map': Tristan Gooley, *The Secret World of Weather* (London: Hodder and Stoughton, 2021), p. 247.

page 68 'Celtic Rainforests Wales project': https://celticrainforests.wales

page 68 'narratives that flicker in and out of time': Cooper, *Dreams and Wishes*, p. 81.

page 70 'Ravens are connected to another Welsh king, Bendigeidfran': Sioned Davies, *The Mabinogion: A New Translation* (Oxford: Oxford University Press, 2007), p. 281.

page 70 'a psychic state achievable through geography': Solnit, p. 6.

page 70 'Keats' "negative capability"': https://www.bl.uk/romantics-and-victorians/articles/john-keats-and-negative-capability

page 72 'death would soon come for you': https://www.gutenberg.org/files/20096/20096-h/20096-h.htm

page 72 'a sign of imminent doom': James MacKillop, *Dictionary of Celtic Mythology* (Oxford: Oxford University Press, 1998), p. 109.

page 72 'unique Inner Hag': Sharon Blackie, *Hagitude: Reimagining the Second Half of Life* (London: September Publishing, 2022), p. 294.

page 72 'a poem by fourteenth-century Welsh poet Dafydd ap Gwilym': https://dafyddapgwilym.net/index_eng.php

page 73 'it feels like a malicious one': https://dafyddapgwilym.net/eng/3win.php poem no. 57 translated by Dafydd Johnston

page 75   'ringing increasing as sea levels rise': https://timeandtidebell.org/
aberdyfi-gwynedd

page 75   'far back as the Bronze Age': https://www.bbc.com/travel/
article/20200318-how-a-storm-revealed-a-welsh-kingdom

4: The Haunted In-Between – East Anglian Fens

page 80   'England's largest bay – the Wash': Francis Pryor, *The Fens:
Discovering England's Ancient Depths* (London: Head of Zeus,
2019), p. xiv.

page 80   'shifting wreaths': https://en.wikisource.org/wiki/FolkLore/
Volume_2/Legends_of_the_Lincolnshire_Cars,_Part_1

page 80   'known locally as "roke"': Robert Macfarlane, *Landmarks*
(London: Penguin Random House, 2015), p. 40.

page 80   'reed for thatching': Annie Proulx, *Fen, Bog & Swamp: A Short
History of Peatland Destruction and Its Role in the Climate Crisis*
(London: Harper Collins, 2022), pp. 54–5.

page 81   'drainage had been underway from Saxon times': Francis Pryor,
Home: A Time Traveller's Tales from Britain's Prehistory (London:
Penguin, 2015), p. 194.

page 81   'Cornelius Vermuyden was employed to oversee the work':
James Boyce, *Imperial Mud: The Fight for the Fens* (London: Icon
Books, 2020), p. 39.

page 81   'Fen Tigers': Isabel Sedgwick, *Wicken Fen: a Souvenir Guide*
(Corsham: Park Lane Press (National Trust), 2016), p. 7.

page 82   'tale of the Dead Moon': www.cantab.net/users/michael.
behrend/repubs/balfour_lincs_cars/pages/dead_moon.html

page 82   'a blinding white light flashed and rose up, and the moon
reappeared': Kevin Crossley-Holland, *Between Worlds: Folktales of
Britain and Ireland* (London: Walker Books, 2019), p. 53.

page 83   'As I am now, so one day will ye be': www.cambridgeindependent.
co.uk/news/the-mysterious-case-of-the-cambridgeshire-fen-
slodger-9054338

page 83   'lure the unsuspecting to a watery death':
www.cambridge-news.co.uk/news/history/
cambridgeshires-terrifying-lantern-men-roam-24150833

page 84   'a window onto a lost East Anglian landscape': Sedgwick, p. 3.

page 85   'devoured by blackness': Kevin Crossley-Holland, *The Old
Stories* (London: Colt Books, 1997), p. 44.

page 86   'see their own shadows upon a bank of cloud': http://gutenberg.
          net.au/ebooks06/0605461h.html#c5

page 87   'phantom fishermen of the meres and marshes': William A.
          Dutt, *Highways and Byways in East Anglia* (London: Macmillan &
          Co Ltd, 1901), p. 147.
          https://archive.org/details/cu31924028114423/page/n170/
          mode/1up?ref=ol&view=theater

page 87   '300,000 reeds, planted by volunteers': *Lakenheath Fen – the first
          ten thousand years* (RSPB booklet).

page 87   'need for reed bed habitat': www.rspb.org.uk/
          birds-and-wildlife/wildlife-guides/bird-a-z/bittern/

page 88   'sound-recording of the underwater soundscape
          of Strumpshaw Fen': https://soundcloud.com/
          ffern-astheseasonsturn/march-23

page 88   'Ely Cathedral tower rises up': www.elystandard.co.uk/news/
          23291405.photographer-captures-photo-ely-cathedral-
          shrouded-fog/
          www.cambridge-news.co.uk/news/local-news/gallery/
          gorgeous-photos-show-fog-descending-26070918

page 89   'eel-island': www.cambridge-news.co.uk/news/history/
          ely-only-accessible-boat-known-23464779

page 89   'collected eel rent from the commoners': Boyce, p. 19.

page 90   'brutal executions of the murderers': http://heritagealive.weebly.
          com/black-sheet.html

page 91   'Tiddy Mun without a name, here's water for you. Lift your
          curse!': Crossley-Holland, p. 203.

page 92   'a figure swathed in flowing fog, he was never seen again': www.
          cantab.net/users/michael.behrend/repubs/balfour_lincs_cars/
          pages/tiddy_mun.html

page 92   'attract back to Lakenheath Fen': www.birdguides.com/news/
          lakenheath-fen-rspb-set-for-expansion

page 93   'some degree of flooding in the Fens': Francis Pryor, *The Fens:
          Discovering England's Ancient Depths* (London: Head of Zeus,
          2019), p. 397.

page 93   'archaeological dyke survey': https://archaeology.co.uk/articles/
          features/excavating-ca-archive-francis-pryor.htm

page 94   'swords, daggers, spearheads, brooches, pins, rings, bracelets and
          more': Pryor, p.120.

page 94   'Flag Fen Bronze Age post alignment': Proulx, p. 54.

page 95 'the peaty depths a known inevitability': Francis Pryor, *Flag Fen: A Concise Archaeoguide* (Gunnislake: Boudicca Books, Kindle edition, 2014), p. 484.

page 97 'saw-sedge being harvested at Wicken Fen': Sedgwick, p. 13.

page 97 '"fen-sucked fogs" that Shakespeare references': *William Shakespeare: The Complete Works*, Stanley Wells and Gary Taylor (eds), (Oxford: Oxford University Press, 1988), 'The Tragedy of King Lear', Act 2, Scene 2, p. 957.

5: The Fog Horn – Devon and Cornwall Coast

page 102 'silvery, misty-looking tower': Virginia Woolf, *To The Lighthouse* (1927), (Ware: Wordsworth edition, 1994), p. 135.

page 102 'the lighthouse keeper lived here in the tower': Roger Barrett, *Start Point and its Lighthouse: History, Map and Guide* (Chudleigh: Orchard Publications, 2006, reprinted 2012), p. 21.

page 103 'be seen through more layers of fog': Veronica della Dorra, *Where Light in Darkness Lies: The Story of the Lighthouse* (London: Reaktion Books, 2022), p. 241.

page 104 'blue of distance': Rebecca Solnit, *A Field Guide to Getting Lost* (Edinburgh: Canongate, 2006), p .29.

page 105 'a pattern of sound and silence': Jennifer Lucy Allan, *The Foghorn's Lament: The Disappearing Music of the Coast* (London: White Rabbit, 2021), p. 91.

page 105 'for the fog signal engine room, the elements had won': Barrett, p. 63.

page 106 'wolf-like howling sound that kept ships away': della Dorra, p. 142.

page 106 'alerting sailors to danger': Bella Bathurst, *The Lighthouse Stevensons: The Extraordinary Story of the Building of the Scottish Lighthouses by the Ancestors of Robert Louis Stevenson* (London: Flamingo, 1999), p. 31.

page 106 'one more isolated beacon along the dangerous coast': www.trinityhouse.co.uk/lighthouses-and-lightvessels/wolf-rock-lighthouse

page 111 'Souter Lighthouse Foghorn': www.foghornrequiem.org

page 112 'coastal fog thought to be in decline': www.nytimes.com/interactive/2022/09/14/climate/san-francisco-fog.html

page 113 'among the shoreline flotsam': Wyl Menmuir, *The Draw of the Sea* (London: Aurum, 2022) p. 23.

page 113 'murderous figures waiting on the shore': Cathryn Pearce,

Cornish Wrecking 1700–1860: Reality and Popular Myth
(Woodbridge: The Boydell Press, 2010), p. 213.

page 114   'decreasing visibility that turned to "dank fog"': Daphne du
Maurier, *Vanishing Cornwall* (London: Penguin Books, 1967), p. 145.

page 114   'clings around her "like a spider's web"': Daphne du Maurier,
Jamaica Inn (1936), (London: Virago), p. 284.

page 115   'sad, symbolic of a vanishing age': Daphne du Maurier, *Vanishing
Cornwall*, p. 59.

page 118   'fog in itself does not muffle sound': Allan, p. 70.

6: Scent of the Sea – East Coast of Scotland

page 123   'human-caused warming exacerbates the effects of El
Niño': www.theguardian.com/environment/2023/jun/15/
record-temperatures-global-heating

page 124   'attachment to the haar "creates strong connections of local
identity"': Benjamin Morris, 'Air Today, Gone Tomorrow:
the Haar of Scotland and Local Atmosphere as Heritage Sites',
International Journal of Intangible Heritage, vol. 8, 2013, p. 96.

page 124   'climate mitigation efforts': Morris, p. 97.

page 125   'human waste was emptied into the streets each evening':
www.edinburghlive.co.uk/news/edinburgh-news/
edinburghs-stinky-history-city-always-18778331

page 125   'smelliest city in the world': www.thrillist.com/travel/nation/
stinkiest-cities-in-the-world

page 125   'a visual representation of Edinburgh's unique and
not unpleasant smellscape': https://sensorymaps.
com/?projects=smells-of-auld-reekie

page 126   'fraoch is based on a Gaelic recipe': 'Heather Ale' by Steve
McGrail: *The Scots Magazine*, November 1996, p. 523.

page 127   'heather and some unknown kind of fog': www.independent.
co.uk/life-style/a-little-bit-of-heather-and-a-special-kind-of-
fog-1308984.html

page 127   'harvest fog as a source of water': https://www.bbc.com/future/
article/20200221-how-fog-can-solve-water-shortage-from-
climate-change-in-peru

page 127   'fog's old meaning of moss or lichen': https://dsl.ac.uk/entry/
snd/fog

page 128   'as if the world can come not only close against us': Alice

Tarbuck, *A Spell in the Wild: A Year (and Six Centuries) of Magic* (London: Two Roads, 2020), p. 5.

page 128 'how to court them, how to cause them': Tarbuck, p. 6.

page 129 'courting a weather pattern makes the world magic': www.youtube.com/watch?v=_GwxqSb_wK0

page 130 'finding a gleaming sprig of St John's Wort': Nan Shepherd, *The Living Mountain* (London: Canongate, 2014), p. 45.

page 130 'Wiccan weather spells suggest their usage for fog-summoning': www.wiccangathering.com/gb/wiccan-spells-for-the-weather/

page 131 'sea fog will "swallow everything you know"': Tarbuck, p. 149.

page 134 'a hideous perpetual drowning': https://www.bbc.co.uk/programmes/m001mc4p

page 134 'witch trials were held in both Denmark and Scotland': Marion Gibson, *Witchcraft: A History in 13 Trials* (London: Simon & Schuster, 2023), p. 27.

page 135 'People smelled the smoke': Gibson, p. 42.

page 135 'Fair is foul, and foul is fair': *William Shakespeare: The Complete Works*, Stanley Wells and Gary Taylor (eds), (Oxford: Oxford University Press, 1988), *Macbeth*, Act 1, Scene 1, p. 977.

page 135 'sailing "in a sieve"': Wells and Taylor, *Macbeth*, Act 1, Scene 3, p. 978.

page 135 'the meeting in North Berwick Church': Gibson, p. 39.

page 136 'effects of climate change [. . .] out of control': www.theguardian.com/environment/2023/jul/07/un–climate-change-hottest-week-world

page 137 'defence against enchantment': https://treesforlife.org.uk/into-the-forest/trees-plants-animals/trees/rowan/rowan-mythology-and-folklore/

page 138 'long feathery masses of crystalline snow': Northern Books, *Ben Nevis and Its Observatory* (Ellon: Famedram Publishers, 2005), p. 22.

page 139 'This deep, gloomy gorge': Northern Books, p. 31.

page 139 'a mere dark speck in the centre': Ibid.

page 139 'an invention known as a "cloud chamber"' : https://www.bbc.co.uk/news/uk-scotland-20608377

page 139 'Nobel Prize in 1927': Marjory Roy, *The Weathermen of Ben Nevis 1883–1904* (Fort William: The Royal Meteorological Society, 2004), p. 4.

page 140 'the crunch of footsteps following them': https://en.wikipedia.org/wiki/Am_Fear_Liath_Mòr (accessed 1/10/23) page 141   'thin mist': Shepherd, p. 44.

page 141   '"ghastl[y] white" fog': Shepherd, p. 17.

page 141   'driving mist': Shepherd, p. 79.

page 141   'transparent mist': Shepherd, p. 99.

page 141   'mistrust of "glamourie"': www.dsl.ac.uk/entry/snd/glamourie

page 143   'enmeshed – fully present, consciously engaged': Sharon Blackie, *The Enchanted Life: Reclaiming the Magic and Wisdom of the Natural World* (London: September Publishing, 2018), p. 151.

page 144   'actualities': www.theguardian.com/lifeandstyle/2019/dec/19/alice-oswald-exclusive-poem-mist

7: Sensing Other Worlds – Beara Peninsula, Ireland

page 147   'Into The Misty': Brian Hinton, *Celtic Crossroads: The Art of Van Morrison* (London: Sanctuary, 2000), p. 108.

page 149   'a writer is always writing': Shirley Jackson, 'Memory and Delusion', *New Yorker*, 31 July 2015. https://www.newyorker.com/books/page-turner/memory-and-delusion

page 150   'make us feel something larger than ourselves': Kerri ní Dochartaigh, *Thin Places* (London: Canongate, 2021), p. 23.

page 150   'the Otherworld is a "realm beyond the senses"': James MacKillop, *Dictionary of Celtic Mythology* (Oxford: Oxford University Press, 1998), p. 317.

page 152   'with sparkling crystal chairs': Mark Williams, *Ireland's Immortals: A History of the Gods of Irish Myth* (Princetown: Princetown University Press, 2016), p. 213.

page 153   'It is Manannán mac Lir who was said to have first given the power': MacKillop, p. 285.

page 153   'Manannan's cloak': www.ernestjournal.co.uk/blog/2015/6/29/manannns-cloak

page 153   'the Cailleach, an elder deity of Irish and Scottish mythology': MacKillop, p. 62.

page 153   'Queen of Winter – presiding over the dark months': Sharon Blackie *If Women Rose Rooted: A Life Changing Journey to Authenticity and Belonging* (London: September Publishing, 2019), pp. 317–18.

page 158   'Battle of Kinsale': www.irishexaminer.com/property/homeandgardens/arid-30870898.html

page 158   'created by the Cailleach': www.irishexaminer.com/lifestyle/
artsandculture/arid-40189209.html

page 158–9 'A fog signal operated on the rock': www.irishlights.ie/tourism/
our-lighthouses/bull-rock.aspx

page 159   'Donn is a lonely god of the Otherworld': MacKillop, p. 131.

page 159   'reached by means of travelling through a lake or cave':
MacKillop, p. 317.

page 160   'the original shape-shifter': Annie Proulx, *Fen, Bog & Swamp:
A Short History of Peatland Destruction and Its Role in the Climate
Crisis* (London: Harper Collins, 2022), p. 75.

page 160   'began to be labelled an "imaginary" island': https://blogs.loc.
gov/maps/2020/06/hy-brasil-the-supernatural-island

page 160   'layers of carbon-storing Sphagnum': Proulx, p. 91.

page 161   'Beara Rainforest': https://beararainforest.com

page 161   'absorb water vapour directly from the atmosphere': Robin Wall
Kimmerer, *Gathering Moss: A Natural and Cultural History of
Mosses* (Dublin: Penguin Random House, 2003), p. 149.

page 162   'an ancient conversation going on between mosses and rocks':
Wall Kimmerer, p. 5.

page 164   'what it means to be home in water': Easkey Britton, *Ebb and
Flow: Connect with the Patterns and Power of Water* (London:
Watkins, 2023), p. 23.

page 164   'the concept of the "memory of water"': Britton, p. 8.

8: The Flavour of Fog – River Thames

page 169   'Fog everywhere': Charles Dickens, *Bleak House* (1853),
(London: Penguin Classics, 1996), p. 13.

page 170   'irretrievably tied to the presence of the tidal river': Peter
Ackroyd, *Thames: Sacred River* (London: Vintage, 2008), p. 71.

page 171   'the foggy winter city as "unreal"': T.S. Eliot, *The Waste Land
and other poems* (London: Faber & Faber, 1940), p. 25.

page 172   '"misty black" gathered at the dead centre': Peter Ackroyd,
Colours of London: A History (London: Frances Lincoln, 2022),
p. 75.

page 172   'The yellow colour': Christine L. Corton, *London Fog: The
Biography* (London: The Belknap Press, 2015), p. 16.

page 172   'pea soup': Corton, p. 18.

page 173   'the evening mist clothes the riverside with poetry': quoted in

Evan R. Firestone, *Mist and Fog in British and European Painting: Fuseli, Friedrich, Turner, Monet and their Contemporaries* (London: Lund Humphries, 2023), p. 118.

page 173   'the mysterious loveliness of such effects': Oscar Wilde, *The Decay of Lying & Other Essays* (London: Penguin Classics, 2010), pp. 27–28.

page 174   'Yesterday there was sun, with an exquisite mist': Letter from Claude Monet to Alice Monet quoted in Sylvie Patin, *Claude Monet in Great Britain*, transl. Maev de la Guardia (TOTAL/Hazan: Paris, 1994).
https://www.tate.org.uk/tate-etc/issue-41-autumn-2017/claude-monet-i-find-london-lovelier-paint-each-day

page 174   'Without the fog, London would not be a beautiful city': quoted by Firestone, p. 135.

page 175   'waterside terrain including shipping': www.tate.org.uk/art/research-publications/jmw-turner/mouth-of-the-thames-sketchbook-r1181357

page 175   'Conrad's literary technique': Firestone, p. 130.

page 175   'a benign immensity of unstained light': Joseph Conrad, *Heart of Darkness* (London: Penguin, 1995), p. 16.

page 176   'the very end of the world, a sea the colour of lead': Conrad, p. 19.

page 176   cold, fog, tempests, disease, exile and death': Ibid.

page 176   'one of the dark places of the earth': Conrad, p. 18.

page 178   'White, wet clouds, which swept by in ghostly fashion': Bram Stoker, *Dracula* (Hertfordshire: Wordsworth Editions, 1993), p. 65.

page 178   'a thin streak of white mist': Stoker, p. 214.

page 178   'shine on me through the fog like two red eyes': Stoker, p. 215.

page 179   'metaphorical parallel between the mythology of Dracula': Rachel Lichtenstein, *Estuary: Out from London to the Sea* (London: Penguin. 2016), p. 197.

page 179   'a place of mystery and of enchantment': Peter Ackroyd, *Thames: Sacred River* (London: Vintage, 2008), p. 395.

page 180   'quite literally the mists of time': Laura Maiklem, *Mudlarking: Lost and Found on the River Thames* (London: Bloomsbury, 2019), p. 63.

page 180   'River Jim who found items out in the marshes': Lichtenstein, p. 217.

page 181   'there were fogs and the cries of frogs and waterbirds': Annie
         Proulx, *Fen, Bog & Swamp: A Short History of Peatland Destruction
         and Its Role in the Climate Crisis* (London: Harper Collins, 2022),
         p. 45.

page 181   'highly effective carbon sinks': www.wwt.org.uk/
         discover-wetlands/wetlands/saltmarsh

page 181   'the atmosphere in this region is always gloomy': https://
         penelope.uchicago.edu/~grout/encyclopaedia_romana/
         britannia/miscellanea/geography.html

page 182   'a city of ghosts; you feel them here': https://www.nytimes.
         com/2012/04/29/travel/a-profile-of-london-by-aa-gill.html

page 183   'ordinary streets in a ghostly twilight haze': Elizabeth Dearnley,
         (Ed.), *Into the London Fog: Eerie Tales from the Weird City*
         (London: The British Library, 2020), p. 9.

page 183   'floating islands of pale light': Virginia Woolf, 'Street Haunting'
         (1927), in Dearnley (Ed.), p. 136.

page 183–4 'the narrator of "Street Haunting" receives a glimpse of the
         shade of her past self': Woolf (1927), in Dearnley (Ed.), p. 146.

page 185   'she enters to find it "full of fog"': Marie Belloc Lowde, 'The
         Lodger' in Dearnley (Ed.), pp. 201, 215.

page 185   'I couldn't stay down there': Ibid.

page 185–6 'the fog came pouring in at every chink and keyhole': Charles
         Dickens, *A Christmas Carol* (1843), (London: Scholastic,
         2016), p. 4.

page 186   'leaving nothing but "sweet fresh air"': Dickens, p. 119.

page 186   'low, level, marshy field, fringed with factories and taverns':
         www.djo.org.uk/household-words/volume-vii/page-273.html

page 186   'the city's inhabitants stoked their fires': Corton, p. 280.

page 186   'inhabitants could not even see their own feet': www.metoffice.
         gov.uk/weather/learn-about/weather/case-studies/great-
         smog#:~:text=During%20the%20period%20of%20the,14%20
         tonnes%20of%20fluorine%20compounds

page 187   'Thames was frozen so solid': Peter Ackroyd, *Thames: Sacred
         River* (London: Vintage, 2008), p. 229.

page 188   'the last Thames frost fair ever held': www.thames.me.uk/
         Frostiana.htm

page 189   'the boundary between the visible and invisible realms':
         Ackroyd, p. 36.

9: Transformed by the Fog – Venice, Italy

page 194   '*nebbia, nebbietta, foschia, caligo*': Paolo Barbaro, (trans. Tami Calliope), *Venice Revealed: An Intimate Portrait* (London: Souvenir Press, 2001), p. 121.

page 196   'water is the image of time': Joseph Brodsky, *Watermark: An Essay on Venice* (London: Penguin, 1992), p. 43.

page 196   'the upright lace of Venetian facades': Ibid.

page 198   'the bridge between human spaces': Giulia Repetti, 'Seven Steps: Water Staircases as Proxies for the Anthropocene in Venice', in Cristina Baldacci, Shaul Bassi, Lucio De Capitani, Pietro Daniel Omedo (eds.), *Venice and the Anthropocene: An Ecocritical Guide* (Venice: Wetlands Books, 2022), p. 81.

page 199   'her floating casket is lit by candles': Alberto Toso Fei (trans. O. Barmine), *Venetian Legends and Ghost Stories: A Guide to Places of Mystery in Venice* (Treviso: Elzeviro, 2004), p. 31.

page 199   'The death-boat chugs away through the mist': Jan Morris, *Venice* (London: Faber & Faber, 1993), p.144.

page 199   'It's evening, it's foggy, the night's about to end': Barbaro, p. 121.

page 201   'Phenomena that are said to characterise the Anthropocene': Baldacci et al, p. 9.

page 202   'a painting that has been described as being about both progress and loss': Evan R. Firestone, *Mist and Fog in British and European Painting: Fuseli, Friedrich, Turner, Monet and their Contemporaries* (London: Lund Humphries, 2023), p. 111.

page 203   'a private light': Brodsky, p. 81.

page 204   'too much splendour seriously damages your health': Tiziano Scarpa, (trans. Shaun Whiteside), *Venice is a Fish: A Cultural Guide* (London: Serpent's Tail, 2008), p. 74.

page 204   '"beauty-clouded" eyes': Scarpa, p. 77.

page 204   'to pass through it is to leave a tunnel behind you': Brodsky, p. 59.

page 204   'when you walk back across Dorsoduro': Morris, p. 185.

page 205   'do as the old woman does': https://archive.nytimes.com/www.nytimes.com/books/97/07/20/reviews/jong-magazine.html

page 206   'the poor innocent baker-boy's bloody revenge': Toso Fei, p. 141.

page 206   'rearrange themselves dextrously': Lauren Elkin, *Flâneuse: Women Walk the City in Paris, New York, Tokyo, Venice and London* (London: Vintage, 2016), p. 135.

page 206   '*Getting lost* is the only place worth going to': Scarpa, p. 7.

page 206   'walking was a way to "shed the self"': Virginia Woolf, 'Street Haunting' (1927), in Elizabeth Dearnley (Ed.), *Into the London Fog: Eerie Tales from the Weird City* (London: The British Library), p. 135.

page 206   'getting lost was not a matter of geography so much as identity': Rebecca Solnit, *A Field Guide to Getting Lost* (Edinburgh: Canongate, 2006), p. 16.

page 207   'The consequences are chilling and horrific': Daphne du Maurier, *Don't Look Now* [1971] *and Other Stories* (London: Penguin Modern Classics, 2006), p. 55.

page 208   'tinkling of the bell-buoys out in the lagoon': Morris, p. 177.

page 208   'you can listen to the fog': Scarpa, p. 51.

page 208   'ancient lagoonal mists': Barbaro, p. 82.

page 209   'among his most vaporous watercolours': Firestone, p. 106.

page 209   'The luminosity of the Venetian paintings': Firestone, p. 107.

page 211   'the hour of unreality': E. M. Forster, *A Room With A View* (1908), (London: Penguin Books), p. 61.

Epilogue

page 218   'like the fog in Alice Oswald's poem': www.theguardian.com/lifeandstyle/2019/dec/19/alice-oswald-exclusive-poem-mist

page 222   'a fog photographer I connected with on Instagram': www.instagram.com/sambinding

page 223   'the old, strong magic of being spoken aloud': Robert Macfarlane and Jackie Morris, *The Lost Words* (London: Hamish Hamilton, 2017), p. 2.

Acknowledgements

I offer my heartfelt thanks to the following people, without whom this book would not exist:

To my wonderful agent, Caroline Hardman, who has been with me every step of the way.

To the brilliant team at Simon & Schuster – particularly my fantastic editor, Fran Jessop, who immediately saw the magic in fog, and who brought this book into being. To copy editor Kerri Sharp, who understood fog's mystery, to designer Pip Watkins for the cover of dreams, to Harriett Collins, Genevieve Barratt, and to everyone else who has worked on this book.

To Sarah Rigby for her superlative writing guidance.

To Rebecca Schiller and the Mothers Who Write community – so much of this book was drafted during our writing sessions; I'm glad to have you on the other side of the screen.

To incredible photographer Jules Williams (@thisisjules) for the perfect author portraits.

To my artist friend Rich Edwards (@richedwardsart) for telling me about the keeper of the lights, and for painting my favourite foggy scenes.

To Meg Adnams of the St Arilda's Church History Society for helping me to find Percy's grave.

To my dear colleagues at the Cotswold Book Room – especially Cathy and Gideon – for their ongoing support.

To Sam Binding (@sambinding), Mistographer, for the weather advice.

To everyone who's supported my writing via Substack, and to the mist-loving kindred spirits I've found on Instagram over the years.

To all those who have ever sent me a fog alert – they mean more than you know.

To Tom for showing me Cloud Chambers, and for the photographs of the foggy city – I think the fog is chasing you!

To Mum, Dad and Annie, for keeping me company on my travels and for always believing in me.

Finally, to Dan, Seth, Rowan and Eli. Thank you for understanding why I spend so much time hiding away in the study, for sending me pictures of fog whenever you see it, and for everything, really. I love you.